August Wilson's
The Piano Lesson

A SAMUEL FRENCH ACTING EDITION

SAMUEL
FRENCH
FOUNDED 1830

SAMUELFRENCH.COM
SAMUELFRENCH-LONDON.CO.UK

MUSIC USE NOTE

Licensees are solely responsible for obtaining formal written permission from copyright owners to use copyrighted music in the performance of this play and are strongly cautioned to do so. If no such permission is obtained by the licensee, then the licensee must use only original music that the licensee owns and controls. Licensees are solely responsible and liable for all music clearances and shall indemnify the copyright owners of the play(s) and their licensing agent, Samuel French, against any costs, expenses, losses and liabilities arising from the use of music by licensees. Please contact the appropriate music licensing authority in your territory for the rights to any incidental music.

IMPORTANT BILLING AND CREDIT REQUIREMENTS

If you have obtained performance rights to this title, please refer to your licensing agreement for important billing and credit requirements.

THE PIANO LESSON was initially presented as a staged reading at The Eugene O'Neill Theater Center's 1987 National Playwrights Conference.

THE PIANO LESSON opened at the Yale Repertory Theatre (Lloyd Richards, Artistic Director; Benjamin Mordecai, Managing Director) on November 26, 1987 in New Haven, Connecticut. The production was directed by Lloyd Richards, with set design by E. David Cosier, Jr., costume design by Constanza Romero, lighting design by Christopher Akerlind, and sound design by J. Scott Servheen. The Musical Director was Dwight Andrews. The Production Stage Manager was Maureen F. Gibson, and the Stage Manager was Gwendolyn M. Gilliam. The cast was as follows:

DOAKER . . . . Carl Gordon
BOY WILLIE . . . . Samuel L. Jackson
LYMON . . . . Rocky Carroll
BERNIECE. . . . . Starletta DuPois
MARETHA. . . . . Chenee Johnson,
                        Ylonda Powell (at alternate performances)
AVERY . . . . Tommy Hollis
WINING BOY . . . . Lou Myers
GRACE . . . . Sharon Washington

The Yale Repertory Theatre production of *THE PIANO LESSON* opened at the Huntington Theatre Company (Peter Altman, Producing Director; Michael Maso, Managing Director) on January 9, 1988 in Boston, Massachusetts. It was directed by Lloyd Richards, with set design by E. David Cosier Jr., costume design by Constanza Romero, lighting design by Christopher Akerlind, and sound design by J. Scott Servheen. The Musical Director was Dwight Andrews. The Stage Manager was Gwendolyn M. Gilliam. The cast was as follows:

DOAKER . . . . Carl Gordon
BOY WILLIE . . . . Charles S. Dutton
LYMON . . . . Rocky Carroll
BERNIECE. . . . . Starletta DuPois
MARETHA. . . . . Jaye Skinner
AVERY . . . . Tommy Hollis
WINING BOY . . . . Lou Myers
GRACE . . . . Sharon Washington

THE PIANO LESSON opened on Broadway at the Walter Kerr Theatre on April 16, 1990 in New York City. It was directed by Lloyd Richards, with set design by E. David Cosier, Jr., costume design by Constanza Romero, lighting design by Christopher Akerlind, and sound design by G. Thomas Clark. The Musical Director was Dwight Andrews. The Production Stage Manager was Karen L. Carpenter, and the Stage Manager was Russell Johnson. The cast was as follows:

DOAKER	Carl Gordon
BOY WILLIE	Charles S. Dutton
LYMON	Rocky Carroll
BERNIECE	S. Epatha Merkerson
MARETHA	Apryl R. Foster
AVERY	Tommy Hollis
WINING BOY	Lou Myers
GRACE	Lisa Gay Hamilton

CHARACTERS

DOAKER

BOY WILLIE

LYMON

BERNIECE

MARETHA

AVERY

WINING BOY

GRACE

SETTING

The action of the play takes place in the kitchen and parlor of the house where Doaker Charles lives with his niece, Berniece, and her eleven-year-old daughter, Maretha. The house is sparsely furnished, and although there is evidence of a woman's touch, there is a lack of warmth and vigor. Berniece and Maretha occupy the upstairs rooms. Doaker's room is prominent and opens onto the kitchen. Dominating the parlor is an old upright piano. On the legs of the piano, carved in the manner of African sculpture, are mask-like figures resembling totems. The carvings are rendered with a grace and power of invention that lifts them out of the realm of craftsmanship and into the realm of art. At left is a staircase leading to the upstairs.

For my sisters and brothers:
Freda
Linda
Donna
Edwin
Richard

ACT ONE

Scene One

(The lights come up on the Charles household. It is five o'clock in the morning. The dawn is beginning to announce itself, but there is something in the air that belongs to the night. A stillness that is a portent, a gathering, a coming together of something akin to a storm. There is a loud knock at the door.)

BOY WILLIE. *(offstage, calling)* Hey, Doaker...Doaker! *(Knocks again and calls)* Hey, Doaker! Hey, Berniece! Berniece!

(DOAKER enters from his room. He is a tall, thin man of forty-seven, with severe features, who has for all intents and purposes retired from the world, though he works full time as a railroad cook.)

DOAKER. Who is it?

BOY WILLIE. Open the door, nigger! It's me...Boy Willie!

DOAKER. Who?

BOY WILLIE. Boy Willie! Open the door!

(DOAKER opens the door and BOY WILLIE and LYMON enter. BOY WILLIE is thirty years old. He has an infectious grin and a boyishness that is apt for his name. He is brash and impulsive, talkative and somewhat crude in speech and manner. LYMON is twenty-nine. BOY WILLIE's partner, he talks little, and then with a straightforwardness that is often disarming.)

DOAKER. What you doing up here?

BOY WILLIE. I told you, Lymon. Lymon talking about you might be sleep. This is Lymon. You remember Lymon Jackson from down home? This my Uncle Doaker.

DOAKER. What you doing up here? I couldn't figure out who that was. I thought you was still down in Mississippi.

BOY WILLIE. Me and Lymon selling watermelons. We got a truck out there. Got a whole truckload of watermelons. We brought them up here to sell. Where's Berniece? *(calls)* Hey, Berniece!

DOAKER. Berniece up there sleep.

BOY WILLIE. Well, let her get up. *(calls)* Hey, Berniece!

DOAKER. She got to go to work in the morning.

BOY WILLIE. Well, she can get up and say hi. It's been three years since I seen her. *(calls)* Hey, Berniece! It's me... Boy Willie.

DOAKER. Berniece don't like all that hollering now. She got to work in the morning.

BOY WILLIE. She can go on back to bed. Me and Lymon been riding two days in that truck...the least she can do is get up and say hi.

DOAKER. *(looking out the window)* Where you all get that truck from?

BOY WILLIE. It's Lymon's. I told him let's get a load of watermelons and bring them up here.

LYMON. Boy Willie say he going back, but I'm gonna stay. See what it's like up here.

BOY WILLIE. You gonna carry me down there first.

LYMON. I told you I ain't going back down there and take a chance on that truck breaking down again. You can take the train. Hey, tell him, Doaker, he can take the train back. After we sell them watermelons he have enough money he can buy him a whole railroad car.

DOAKER. You got all them watermelons stacked up there no wonder the truck broke down. I'm surprised you made it this far with a load like that. Where you break down at?

BOY WILLIE. We broke down three times! It took us two and a half days to get here. It's a good thing we picked them watermelons fresh.

LYMON. We broke down twice in West Virginia. The first time was just as soon as we got out of Sunflower. About forty miles out she broke down. We got it going and got all the way to West Virginia before she broke down again.

BOY WILLIE. We had to walk about five miles for some water.

LYMON. It got a hole in the radiator but it runs pretty good. You have to pump the brakes sometime before they catch. Boy Willie have his door open and be ready to jump when that happens.

BOY WILLIE. Lymon think that's funny. I told the nigger I give him ten dollars to get the brakes fixed. But he thinks that funny.

LYMON. They don't need fixing. All you got to do is pump them till they catch.

> *(**BERNIECE** enters on the stairs. Thirty-five years old, with an eleven-year-old daughter, she is still in mourning for her husband after three years.)*

BERNIECE. What you doing all that hollering for?

BOY WILLIE. Hey Berniece. Doaker said you was sleep. I said at least you could get up and say hi.

BERNIECE. It's five o'clock in the morning and you come in here with all this noise. You can't come like normal folks. You got to bring all that noise with you.

BOY WILLIE. Hell, I ain't done nothing but come in and say hi. I ain't got in the house good.

BERNIECE. That's what I'm talking about. You start all that hollering and carry on as soon as you hit the door.

BOY WILLIE. Aw hell, woman, I was glad to see Doaker. You ain't had to come down if you didn't want to. I come eighteen hundred miles to see my sister I figure she might want to get up and say hi. Other than that you can go back upstairs. What you got, Doaker? Where your bottle? Me and Lymon want a drink. *(to* **BERNIECE***)* This is Lymon. You remember Lymon Jackson from down home.

LYMON. How you doing, Berniece. You look just like I thought you looked.

BERNIECE. Why you all got to come in hollering and carrying on? Waking the neighbors with all that noise.

BOY WILLIE. They can come over and join the party. We fixing to have a party. Doaker, where your bottle? Me and Lymon celebrating. The Ghosts of the Yellow Dog got Sutter.

BERNIECE. Say what?

BOY WILLIE. Ask Lymon, they found him the next morning. Say he drowned in his well.

DOAKER. When this happen, Boy Willie?

BOY WILLIE. About three weeks ago. Me and Lymon was over in Stoner County when we heard about it. We laughed. We thought it was funny. A great big old three-hundred-and-forty-pound man gonna fall down his well.

LYMON. It remind me of Humpty Dumpty.

BOY WILLIE. Everybody say the Ghosts of the Yellow Dog pushed him.

BERNIECE. I don't want to hear that nonsense. Somebody down there pushing them people in their wells.

DOAKER. What was you and Lymon doing over in Stoner County?

BOY WILLIE. We was down there working. Lymon got some people down there.

LYMON. My cousin got some land down there. We was helping him.

BOY WILLIE. Got near about a hundred acres. He got it set up real nice. Me and Lymon was down there chopping down trees. We was using Lymon's truck to haul the wood. Me and Lymon used to haul wood all around them parts. *(to* **BERNIECE***)* Me and Lymon got a truckload of watermelons out there.

*(**BERNIECE** crosses to the window to the parlor.)*

Doaker, where your bottle? I know you got a bottle stuck up in your room. Come on, me and Lymon want a drink.

*(**DOAKER** exits into his room.)*

BERNIECE. Where you all get that truck from?

BOY WILLIE. I told you it's Lymon's.

BERNIECE. Where you get the truck from, Lymon?

LYMON. I bought it.

BERNIECE. Where he get that truck from, Boy Willie?

BOY WILLIE. He told you he bought it. Bought it for a hundred and twenty dollars. I can't say where he got that hundred and twenty dollars from…but he bought that old piece of truck from Henry Porter. *(to* **LYMON***)* Where you get that hundred and twenty dollars from, nigger?

LYMON. I got it like you get yours. I know how to take care of money.

*(**DOAKER** brings a bottle and sets it on the table.)*

BOY WILLIE. Aw hell, Doaker got some of that good whiskey. Don't give Lymon none of that. He ain't used to good whiskey. He liable to get sick.

LYMON. I done had good whiskey before.

BOY WILLIE. Lymon bought that truck so he have him a place to sleep. He down there wasn't doing no work or nothing. Sheriff looking for him. He bought that truck to keep away from the sheriff. Got Stovall looking for him too. He down there sleeping in that truck ducking and dodging both of them. I told him come on let's go up and see my sister.

BERNIECE. What the sheriff looking for you for, Lymon?

BOY WILLIE. The man don't want you to know all his business. He's my company. He ain't asking you no questions.

LYMON. It wasn't nothing. It was just a misunderstanding.

BERNIECE. He in my house. You say the sheriff looking for him, I wanna know what he looking for him for. Otherwise you all can go back out there and be where nobody don't have to ask you nothing.

LYMON. It was just a misunderstanding. Sometimes me and the sheriff we don't think alike. So we just got crossed on each other.

BERNIECE. Might be looking for him about that truck. He might have stole that truck.

BOY WILLIE. We ain't stole no truck, woman. I told you Lymon bought it.

DOAKER. Boy Willie and Lymon got more sense than to ride all the way up here in a stolen truck with a load of watermelons. Now they might have stole them watermelons, but I don't believe they stole that truck.

BOY WILLIE. You don't even know the man good and you calling him a thief. And we ain't stole them watermelons either. Them old man Pitterford's watermelons. He give me and Lymon all we could load for ten dollars.

DOAKER. No wonder you got them stacked up out there. You must have five hundred watermelons stacked up out there.

BERNIECE. Boy Willie, when you and Lymon planning on going back?

BOY WILLIE. Lymon say he staying. As soon as we sell them watermelons I'm going on back.

BERNIECE. (*starts to exit up the stairs*) That's what you need to do. And you need to do it quick. Come in here disrupting the house. I don't want all that loud carrying on around here. I'm surprised you ain't woke Maretha up.

BOY WILLIE. I was fixing to get her now. (*calls*) Hey, Maretha!

DOAKER. Berniece don't like all that hollering now.

BERNIECE. Don't you wake that child up!

BOY WILLIE. You going up there…wake her up and tell her her uncle's here. I ain't seen her in three years. Wake her up and send her down here. She can go back to bed.

BERNIECE. I ain't waking that child up…and don't you be making all that noise. You and Lymon need to sell them watermelons and go on back.

(**BERNIECE** *exits up the stairs.*)

BOY WILLIE. I see Berniece still try to be stuck up.

DOAKER. Berniece all right. She don't want you making all that noise. Maretha up there sleep. Let her sleep until she get up. She can see you then.

BOY WILLIE. I ain't thinking about Berniece. You hear from Wining Boy? You know Cleotha died?

DOAKER. Yeah, I heard that. He come by here about a year ago. Had a whole sack of money. He stayed here about two weeks. Ain't offered nothing. Berniece asked him for three dollars to buy some food and he got mad and left.

LYMON. Who's Wining Boy?

BOY WILLIE. That's my uncle. That's Doaker's brother. You heard me talk about Wining Boy. He play piano. He done made some records and everything. He still doing that, Doaker?

DOAKER. He made one or two records a long time ago. That's the only ones I ever known him to make. If you let him tell it he a big recording star.

BOY WILLIE. He stopped down home about two years ago. That's what I hear. I don't know. Me and Lymon was up on Parchman Farm doing them three years.

DOAKER. He don't never stay in one place. Now, he been here about eight months ago. Back in the winter. Now, you subject not to see him for another two years. It's liable to be that long before he stop by.

BOY WILLIE. If he had a whole sack of money you liable never to see him. You ain't gonna see him until he get broke. Just as soon as that sack of money is gone you look up and he be on your doorstep.

LYMON. *(noticing the piano)* Is that the piano?

BOY WILLIE. Yeah…look here, Lymon. See how it got all those carvings on it. See, that's what I was talking about. See how it's carved up real nice and polished and everything? You never find you another piano like that.

LYMON. Yeah, that look real nice.

BOY WILLIE. I told you. See how it's polished? My mama used to polish it every day. See all them pictures carved on it? That's what I was talking about. You can get a nice price for that piano.

LYMON. That's all Boy Willie talked about the whole trip up here. I got tired of hearing him talk about the piano.

BOY WILLIE. All you want to talk about is women. You ought to hear this nigger, Doaker. Talking about all the women he gonna get when he get up here. He ain't had none down there but he gonna get a hundred when he get up here.

DOAKER. How your people doing down there, Lymon?

LYMON. They all right. They still there. I come up here to see what it's like up here. Boy Willie trying to get me to go back and farm with him.

BOY WILLIE. Sutter's brother selling the land. He say he gonna sell it to me. That's why I come up here. I got one part of it. Sell them watermelons and get me another part. Get Berniece to sell that piano and I'll have the third part.

DOAKER. Berniece ain't gonna sell that piano.

BOY WILLIE. I'm gonna talk to her. When she see I got a chance to get Sutter's land she'll come around.

DOAKER. You can put that thought out your mind. Berniece ain't gonna sell that piano.

BOY WILLIE. I'm gonna talk to her. She been playing on it?

DOAKER. You know she won't touch that piano. I ain't never known her to touch it since Mama Ola died. That's over seven years now. She say it got blood on it. She got Maretha playing on it though. Say Maretha can go on and do everything she can't do. Got her in an extra school down at the Irene Kaufman Settlement House. She want Maretha to grow up and be a schoolteacher. Say she good enough she can teach on the piano.

BOY WILLIE. Maretha don't need to be playing on no piano. She can play on the guitar.

DOAKER. How much land Sutter got left?

BOY WILLIE. Got a hundred acres. Good land. He done sold it piece by piece, he kept the good part for himself. Now he got to give that up. His brother come down from Chicago for the funeral…he up there in Chicago got some kind of business with soda fountain equipment. He anxious to sell the land, Doaker. He don't want to be bothered with it. He called me to him and said 'cause of how long our families done known each other and how we been good friends and all, say he wanted to sell the land to me. Say he'd rather see me with it than Jim Stovall. Told me he'd let me have it for two thousand dollars cash money. He don't know I found out the most Stovall would give him for it was fifteen hundred dollars. He trying to get that extra five hundred out of me telling me he doing me a favor. I thanked him just as nice. Told him what a good man Sutter was and how he had my sympathy and all. Told him to give me two weeks. He said he'd wait on me. That's why I come up here. Sell them watermelons. Get Berniece to sell that piano. Put them two parts with the part I done saved. Walk in there. Tip my hat. Lay my money down on the table. Get my deed and walk on out. This time I get to keep all the cotton. Hire me some men to work it for me. Gin my cotton. Get my seed. And I'll see you again next year. Might even plant some tobacco or some oats.

DOAKER. You gonna have a hard time trying to get Berniece to sell that piano. You know Avery Brown from down there don't you? He up here now. He followed Berniece up here trying to get her to marry him after Crawley got killed. He been up here about two years. He call himself a preacher now.

BOY WILLIE. I know Avery. I know him from when he used to work on the Willshaw place. Lymon know him too.

DOAKER. He after Berniece to marry him. She keep telling him no but he won't give up. He keep pressing her on it.

BOY WILLIE. Avery think all white men is big shots. He don't know there some white men ain't got as much as he got.

DOAKER. He supposed to come past here this morning. Berniece going down to the bank with him to see if he can get a loan to start his church. That's why I know Berniece ain't gonna sell that piano. He tried to get her to sell it to help him start his church. Sent the man around and everything.

BOY WILLIE. What man?

DOAKER. Some white fellow was going around to all the colored people's houses looking to buy up musical instruments. He'd buy anything. Drums. Guitars. Harmonicas. Pianos. Avery sent him past here. He looked at the piano and got excited. Offered her a nice price. She turned him down and got on Avery for sending him past. The man kept on her about two weeks. He seen where she wasn't gonna sell it, he gave her his number and told her if she ever wanted to sell it to call him first. Say he'd do one better than what anybody else would give her for it.

BOY WILLIE. How much he offer her for it?

DOAKER. Now you know me. She didn't say and I didn't ask. I just know it was a nice price.

LYMON. All you got to do is find out who he is and tell him somebody else wanna buy it from you. Tell him you can't make up your mind who to sell it to, and if he like Doaker say, he'll give you anything you want for it.

BOY WILLIE. That's what I'm gonna do. I'm gonna find out who he is from Avery.

DOAKER. It ain't gonna do you no good. Berniece ain't gonna sell that piano.

BOY WILLIE. She ain't got to sell it. I'm gonna sell it. I own just as much of it as she does.

BERNIECE. (offstage, hollers) Doaker! Go on get away. Doaker!

DOAKER. (calling) Berniece?

> (**DOAKER** and **BOY WILLIE** rush to the stairs. **BOY WILLIE** runs up the stairs, passing **BERNIECE** as she enters, running.)

Berniece, what's the matter? You all right? What's the matter?

> (**BERNIECE** tries to catch her breath. She is unable to speak.)

That's all right. Take your time. You all right. What's the matter? (calls) Hey, Boy Willie?

BOY WILLIE. (offstage) Ain't nobody up here.

BERNIECE. Sutter…Sutter's standing at the top of the steps.

DOAKER. (calls) Boy Willie!

> (**LYMON** crosses to the stairs and looks up. **BOY WILLIE** enters from the stairs.)

BOY WILLIE. Hey Doaker, what's wrong with her? Berniece, what's wrong? Who was you talking to?

DOAKER. She say she seen Sutter's ghost standing at the top of the stairs.

BOY WILLIE. Seen what? Sutter? She ain't seen no Sutter.

BERNIECE. He was standing right up there.

BOY WILLIE. That's all in Berniece's head. Ain't nobody up there. Go on up there, Doaker.

DOAKER. I'll take your word for it. Berniece talking about what she seen. She say Sutter's ghost standing at the top of the steps. She ain't just make all that up.

BOY WILLIE. She up there dreaming. She ain't seen no ghost.

LYMON. You want a glass of water, Berniece? Get her a glass of water, Boy Willie.

BOY WILLIE. She don't need no water. She ain't seen nothing. Go on up there and look. Ain't nobody up there but Maretha.

DOAKER. Let Berniece tell it.

BOY WILLIE. I ain't stopping her from telling it.

DOAKER. What happened, Berniece?

BERNIECE. I come out my room to come back down here and Sutter was standing there in the hall.

BOY WILLIE. What he look like?

BERNIECE. He look like Sutter. He look like he always look.

BOY WILLIE. Sutter couldn't find his way from Big Sandy to Little Sandy. How he gonna find his way all the way up here to Pittsburgh? Sutter ain't never even heard of Pittsburgh.

DOAKER. Go on, Berniece.

BERNIECE. Just standing there with the blue suit on.

BOY WILLIE. The man ain't never left Marlin County when he was living…and he's gonna come all the way up here now that he's dead?

DOAKER. Let her finish. I want to hear what she got to say.

BOY WILLIE. I'll tell you this. If Berniece had seen him like she think she seen him she'd still be running.

DOAKER. Go on, Berniece. Don't pay Boy Willie no mind.

BERNIECE. He was standing there…had his hand on top of his head. Look like he might have thought if he took his hand down his head might have fallen off.

LYMON. Did he have on a hat?

BERNIECE. Just had on that blue suit...I told him to go away and he just stood there looking at me...calling Boy Willie's name.

BOY WILLIE. What he calling my name for?

BERNIECE. I believe you pushed him in the well.

BOY WILLIE. Now what kind of sense that make? You telling me I'm gonna go out there and hide in the weeds with all them dogs and things he got around there...I'm gonna hide and wait till I catch him looking down his well just right...then I'm gonna run over and push him in. A great big old three-hundred-and-forty-pound man.

BERNIECE. Well, what he calling your name for?

BOY WILLIE. He bending over looking down his well, woman...how he know who pushed him? It could have been anybody. Where was you when Sutter fell in his well? Where was Doaker? Me and Lymon was over in Stoner County. Tell her, Lymon. The Ghosts of the Yellow Dog got Sutter. That's what happened to him.

BERNIECE. You can talk all that Ghosts of the Yellow Dog stuff if you want. I know better.

LYMON. The Ghosts of the Yellow Dog pushed him. That's what the people say. They found him in his well and all the people say it must be the Ghosts of the Yellow Dog. Just like all them other men.

BOY WILLIE. Come talking about he looking for me. What he come all the way up here for? If he looking for me all he got to do is wait. He could have saved himself a trip if he looking for me. That ain't nothing but in Berniece's head. Ain't no telling what she liable to come up with next.

BERNIECE. Boy Willie, I want you and Lymon to go ahead and leave my house. Just go on somewhere. You don't do nothing but bring trouble with you everywhere you go. If it wasn't for you Crawley would still be alive.

BOY WILLIE. Crawley what? I ain't had nothing to do with Crawley getting killed. Crawley three time seven. He had his own mind.

BERNIECE. Just go on and leave. Let Sutter go somewhere else looking for you.

BOY WILLIE. I'm leaving. Soon as we sell them watermelons. Other than that I ain't going nowhere. Hell, I just got here. Talking about Sutter looking for me. Sutter was looking for that piano. That's what he was looking for. He had to die to find out where that piano was at...If I was you I'd get rid of it. That's the way to get rid of Sutter's ghost. Get rid of that piano.

BERNIECE. I want you and Lymon to go on and take all this confusion out of my house!

BOY WILLIE. Hey tell her, Doaker. What kind of sense that make? I told you, Lymon, as soon as Berniece see me she was gonna start something. Didn't I tell you that? Now she done made up that story about Sutter just so she could tell me to leave her house. Well, hell, I ain't going nowhere till I sell them watermelons.

BERNIECE. Well why don't you go out there and sell them! Sell them and go on back!

BOY WILLIE. We waiting till the people get up.

LYMON. Boy Willie say if you get out there too early and wake the people up they get mad at you and won't buy nothing from you.

DOAKER. You won't be waiting long. You done let the sun catch up with you. This the time everybody be getting up around here.

BERNIECE. Come on, Doaker, walk up here with me. Let me get Maretha up and get her started. I got to get ready myself. Boy Willie, just go on out there and sell them watermelons and you and Lymon leave my house.

(**BERNIECE** and **DOAKER** *exit up the stairs.*)

BOY WILLIE. *(calling after them)* If you see Sutter up there... tell him I'm down here waiting on him.

LYMON. What if she see him again?

BOY WILLIE. That's all in her head. There ain't no ghost up there. *(calls)* Hey, Doaker...I told you ain't nothing up there.

LYMON. I'm glad he didn't say he was looking for me.

BOY WILLIE. I wish I would see Sutter's ghost. Give me a chance to put a whupping on him.

LYMON. You ought to stay up here with me. You be down there working his land...he might come looking for you all the time.

BOY WILLIE. I ain't thinking about Sutter. And I ain't thinking about staying up here. You stay up here. I'm going back and get Sutter's land. You think you ain't got to work up here. You think this the land of milk and honey. But I ain't scared of work. I'm going back and farm every acre of that land.

(DOAKER *enters from the stairs.*)

I told you there ain't nothing up there, Doaker. Berniece dreaming all that.

DOAKER. I believe Berniece seen something. Berniece level-headed. She ain't just made all that up. She say Sutter had on a suit. I don't believe she ever seen Sutter in a suit. I believe that's what he was buried in, and that's what Berniece saw.

BOY WILLIE. Well, let her keep on seeing him then. As long as he don't mess with me.

(DOAKER *starts to cook his breakfast.*)

I heard about you, Doaker. They say you got all the women looking out for you down home. They be looking to see you coming. Say you got a different one every two weeks. Say they be fighting one another for you to stay with them. *(to* LYMON*)* Look at him, Lymon. He know it's true.

DOAKER. I ain't thinking about no women. They never get me tied up with them. After Coreen I ain't got no use for them. I stay up on Jack Slattery's place when I be down there. All them women want is somebody with a steady payday.

BOY WILLIE. That ain't what I hear. I hear every two weeks the women all put on their dresses and line up at the railroad station.

DOAKER. I don't get down there but once a month. I used to go down there every two weeks but they keep switching me around. They keep switching all the fellows around.

BOY WILLIE. Doaker can't turn that railroad loose. He was working the railroad when I was walking around crying for sugartit. My mama used to brag on him.

DOAKER. I'm cooking now, but I used to line track. I pieced together the Yellow Dog stitch by stitch. Rail by rail. Line track all up around there. I lined track all up around Sunflower and Clarksdale. Wining Boy worked with me. He helped put in some of that track. He'd work it for six months and quit. Go back to playing piano and gambling.

BOY WILLIE. How long you been with the railroad now?

DOAKER. Twenty-seven years. Now, I'll tell you something about the railroad. What I done learned after twenty-seven years. See, you got North. You got West. You look over here you got South. Over there you got East. Now, you can start from anywhere. Don't care where you at. You got to go one of them four ways. And whichever way you decide to go they got a railroad that will take you there. Now, that's something simple. You think anybody would be able to understand that. But you'd be surprised how many people trying to go North get on a train going West. They think the train's supposed to go where they going rather than where it's going.

Now, why people going? Their sister's sick. They leaving before they kill somebody...and they sitting across from somebody who's leaving to keep from getting killed. They leaving 'cause they can't get satisfied. They going to meet someone. I wish I had a dollar for every time that someone wasn't at the station to meet them.

I done seen that a lot. In between the time they sent the telegram and the time the person get there...they done forgot all about them.

They got so many trains out there they have a hard time keeping them from running into each other. Got trains going every which away. Got people on all of them. Somebody going where somebody just left. If everybody stay in one place I believe this would be a better world. Now what I done learned after twenty-seven years of railroading is this...if the train stays on the track...it's going to get where it's going. It might not be where you going. If it ain't, then all you got to do is sit and wait 'cause the train's coming back to get you. The train don't never stop. It'll come back every time. Now I'll tell you another thing...

BOY WILLIE. What you cooking over there, Doaker? Me and Lymon's hungry.

DOAKER. Go on down there to Wylie and Kirkpatrick to Eddie's restaurant. Coffee cost a nickel and you can get two eggs, sausage and grits for fifteen cents. He even give you a biscuit with it.

BOY WILLIE. That look good what you got. Give me a little piece of that grilled bread.

DOAKER. Here...go on take the whole piece.

BOY WILLIE. Here you go, Lymon...you want a piece?

(He gives **LYMON** *a piece of toast.* **MARETHA** *enters from the stairs.)*

Hey, sugar. Come here and give me a hug. Come on give Uncle Boy Willie a hug. Don't be shy. Look at her, Doaker. She done got bigger. Ain't she got big?

DOAKER. Yeah, she getting up there.

BOY WILLIE. How you doing, sugar?

MARETHA. Fine.

BOY WILLIE. You was just a little old thing last time I seen you. You remember me, don't you? This your Uncle Boy Willie from down South. That there's Lymon. He my friend. We come up here to sell watermelons. You like watermelons?

>   (**MARETHA** *nods.*)

We got a whole truckload out front. You can have as many as you want. What you been doing?

MARETHA. Nothing.

BOY WILLIE. Don't be shy now. Look at you getting all big. How old is you?

MARETHA. Eleven. I'm gonna be twelve soon.

BOY WILLIE. You like it up here? You like the North?

MARETHA. It's all right.

BOY WILLIE. That there's Lymon. Did you say hi to Lymon?

MARETHA. Hi.

LYMON. How you doing? You look just like your mama. I remember you when you was wearing diapers.

BOY WILLIE. You gonna come down South and see me? Uncle Boy Willie gonna get him a farm. Gonna get a great big old farm. Come down there and I'll teach you how to ride a mule. Teach you how to kill a chicken, too.

MARETHA. I seen my mama do that.

BOY WILLIE. Ain't nothing to it. You just grab him by his neck and twist it. Get you a real good grip and then you just wring his neck and throw him in the pot. Cook him up. Then you got some good eating. What you like to eat? What kind of food you like?

MARETHA. I like everything...except I don't like no black-eyed peas.

BOY WILLIE. Uncle Doaker tell me your mama got you playing that piano. Come on play something for me.

>   (**BOY WILLIE** *crosses over to the piano, followed by*
>   **MARETHA**.)

Show me what you can do. Come on now. Here...Uncle Boy Willie give you a dime...show me what you can do. Don't be bashful now. That dime say you can't be bashful.

(MARETHA plays. It is something any beginner first learns.)

Here, let me show you something.

(BOY WILLIE sits and plays a simple boogie-woogie.)

See that? See what I'm doing? That's what you call the boogie-woogie. See now...you can get up and dance to that. That's how good it sound. It sound like you wanna dance. You can dance to that. It'll hold you up. Whatever kind of dance you wanna do you can dance to that right there. See that? See how it go? Ain't nothing to it. Go on you do it.

MARETHA. I got to read it on the paper.

BOY WILLIE. You don't need no paper. Go on. Do just like that there.

BERNIECE. *(offstage, calling)* Maretha! You get up here and get ready to go so you be on time. Ain't no need you trying to take advantage of company.

MARETHA. I got to go.

BOY WILLIE. Uncle Boy Willie gonna get you a guitar. Let Uncle Doaker teach you how to play that. You don't need to read no paper to play the guitar. Your mama told you about that piano? You know how them pictures got on there?

MARETHA. She say it just always been like that since she got it.

BOY WILLIE. You hear that, Doaker? And you sitting up here in the house with Berniece.

DOAKER. I ain't got nothing to do with that. I don't get in the way of Berniece's raising her.

BOY WILLIE. You tell your mama to tell you about that piano. You ask her how them pictures got on there. If she don't tell you I'll tell you.

BERNIECE. *(offstage)* Maretha!

MARETHA. I got to get ready to go.

(exits up the stairs)

BOY WILLIE. She getting big, Doaker. You remember her, Lymon?

LYMON. She used to be real little.

(There is a knock on the door. DOAKER *goes to answer it* AVERY *enters. Thirty-eight years old, honest and ambitious, he has taken to the city like a fish to water, finding in it opportunities for growth and advancement that did not exist for him in the rural South. He is dressed in a suit and tie with a gold cross around his neck. He carries a small Bible.)*

DOAKER. Hey, Avery, come on in. Berniece upstairs.

BOY WILLIE. Look at him…look at him…he don't know what to say. He wasn't expecting to see me.

AVERY. Hey, Boy Willie. What you doing up here?

BOY WILLIE. Look at him, Lymon.

AVERY. Is that Lymon? Lymon Jackson?

BOY WILLIE. Yeah, you know Lymon.

DOAKER. Berniece be ready in a minute, Avery.

BOY WILLIE. Doaker say you a preacher now. What…we supposed to call you Reverend? You used to be plain old Avery. When you get to be a preacher, nigger?

LYMON. Avery say he gonna be a preacher so he don't have to work.

BOY WILLIE. I remember when you was down there on the Willshaw place planting cotton. You wasn't thinking about no Reverend then.

AVERY. That must be your truck out there. I saw that truck with them watermelons, I was trying to figure out what it was doing in front of the house.

BOY WILLIE. Yeah, me and Lymon selling watermelons. That's Lymon's truck.

DOAKER. Berniece say you all going down to the bank.

AVERY. Yeah, they give me a half day off work. I got an appointment to talk to the bank about getting a loan to start my church.

BOY WILLIE. Lymon say preachers don't have to work. Where you working at, nigger?

DOAKER. Avery got him one of them good jobs. He working at one of them skyscrapers downtown.

AVERY. I'm working down there at the Gulf Building running an elevator. Got a pension and everything. They even give you a turkey on Thanksgiving.

LYMON. How you know the rope ain't gonna break? Ain't you scared the rope's gonna break?

AVERY. That's steel. They got steel cables hold it up. It take a whole lot of breaking to break that steel. Naw, I ain't worried about nothing like that. It ain't nothing but a little old elevator. Now, I wouldn't get in none of them airplanes. You couldn't pay me to do nothing like that.

LYMON. That be fun. I'd rather do that than ride in one of them elevators.

BOY WILLIE. How many of them watermelons you wanna buy?

AVERY. I thought you was gonna give me one seeing as how you got a whole truck full.

BOY WILLIE. You can get one, get two. I'll give you two for a dollar.

AVERY. I can't eat but one. How much are they?

BOY WILLIE. Aw, nigger, you know I'll give you a watermelon. Go on, take as many as you want. Just leave some for me and Lymon to sell.

AVERY. I don't want but one.

BOY WILLIE. How you get to be a preacher, Avery? I might want to be a preacher one day. Have everybody call me Reverend Boy Willie.

AVERY. It come to me in a dream. God called me and told me he wanted me to be a shepherd for his flock. That's what I'm gonna call my church...The Good Shepherd Church of God in Christ.

DOAKER. Tell him what you told me. Tell him about the three hoboes.

AVERY. Boy Willie don't want to hear all that.

LYMON. I do. Lots a people say your dreams can come true.

AVERY. Naw. You don't want to hear all that.

DOAKER. Go on. I told him you was a preacher. He didn't want to believe me. Tell him about the three hoboes.

AVERY. Well, it come to me in a dream. See...I was sitting out in this railroad yard watching the trains go by. The train stopped and these three hoboes got off. They told me they had come from Nazareth and was on their way to Jerusalem. They had three candles. They gave me one and told me to light it...but to be careful that it didn't go out. Next thing I knew I was standing in front of this house. Something told me to go knock on the door. This old woman opened the door and said they had been waiting on me. Then she led me into this room. It was a big room and it was full of all kinds of different people. They looked like anybody else except they all had sheep heads and was making noise like sheep make. I heard somebody call my name. I looked around and there was these same three hoboes. They told me to take off my clothes and they give me a blue robe with gold thread. They washed my feet and combed my hair. Then they showed me these three doors and told me to pick one.

I went through one of them doors and that flame leapt off that candle and it seemed like my whole head caught fire. I looked around and there was four or five other men standing there with these same blue robes on. Then we heard a voice tell us to look out across this valley. We looked out and saw the valley was full of wolves. The voice told us that these sheep people that I had seen in the other room had to go over to the other side of this valley and somebody had to take them. Then I heard another voice say "Who shall I send?" Next thing I knew I said, "Here I am. Send me." That's when I met Jesus. He say "If you go, I'll go with you." Something told me to say, "Come on. Let's go."

That's when I woke up. My head still felt like it was on fire...but I had a peace about myself that was hard to explain. I knew right then that I had been filled with the Holy Ghost and called to be a servant of the Lord. It took me a while before I could accept that. But then a lot of little ways God showed me that it was true. So I became a preacher.

LYMON. I see why you gonna call it the Good Shepherd Church. You dreaming about them sheep people. I can see that easy.

BOY WILLIE. Doaker say you sent some white man past the house to look at that piano. Say he was going around to all the colored people's houses looking to buy up musical instruments.

AVERY. Yeah, but Berniece didn't want to sell that piano. After she told me about it...I could see why she didn't want to sell it.

BOY WILLIE. What's this man's name?

AVERY. Oh, that's a while back now. I done forgot his name. He give Berniece a card with his name and telephone number on it, but I believe she throwed it away.

(**BERNIECE** and **MARETHA** enter from the stairs.)

BERNIECE. Maretha, run back upstairs and get my pocketbook. And wipe that hair grease off your forehead. Go ahead, hurry up.

(**MARETHA** exits up the stairs.)

How you doing, Avery? You done got all dressed up. You look nice. Boy Willie, I thought you and Lymon was going to sell them watermelons.

BOY WILLIE. Lymon done got sleepy. We liable to get some sleep first.

LYMON. I ain't sleepy.

DOAKER. As many watermelons as you got stacked up on that truck out there, you ought to have been gone.

BOY WILLIE. We gonna go in a minute. We going.

BERNIECE. Doaker. I'm gonna stop down there on Logan Street. You want anything?

DOAKER. You can pick up some ham hocks if you going down there. See if you can get the smoked ones. If they ain't got that get the fresh ones. Don't get the ones that got all that fat under the skin. Look for the long ones. They nice and lean. *(Gives her a dollar)* Don't get the short ones lessen they smoked. If you got to get the fresh ones make sure that they the long ones. If they ain't got them smoked then go ahead and get the short ones. *(Pause)* You may as well get some turnip greens while you down there. I got some buttermilk...if you pick up some cornmeal I'll make me some cornbread and cook up them turnip greens.

(MARETHA enters from the stairs.)

MARETHA. We gonna take the streetcar?

BERNIECE. Me and avery gonna drop you off at the settlement house. You mind them people down there. Don't be going down there showing your color. Boy Willie, I done told you what to do. I'll see you later, Doaker.

AVERY. I'll be seeing you again, Boy Willie.

BOY WILLIE. Hey, Berniece...what's the name of that man Avery sent past say he want to buy the piano?

BERNIECE. I knew it. I knew it when I first seen you. I knew you was up to something.

BOY WILLIE. Sutter's brother say he selling the land to me. He waiting on me now. Told me he'd give me two weeks. I got one part. Sell them watermelons get me another part. Then we can sell that piano and I'll have the third part.

BERNIECE. I ain't selling that piano, Boy Willie. If that's why you come up here you can just forget about it. *(to* **DOAKER***)* Doaker, I'll see you later. Boy Willie ain't nothing but a whole lot of mouth. I ain't paying him no mind. If he come up here thinking he gonna sell that piano then he done come up here for nothing.

(BERNIECE, AVERY and MARETHA exit out the front door.)

BOY WILLIE. Hey, Lymon! You ready to go sell these watermelons.

(BOY WILLIE and LYMON start to exit. At the door BOY WILLIE turns to DOAKER.)

Hey, Doaker...if Berniece don't want to sell that piano...I'm gonna cut it in half and go on and sell my half.

(BOY WILLIE and LYMON exit. The lights go down on the scene.)

Scene Two

(The lights come up on the kitchen. It is three days later. **WINING BOY** *sits at the kitchen table. There is a half empty pint bottle on the table.* **DOAKER** *busies himself washing pots.* **WINING BOY** *is fifty-six years old.* **DOAKER***'s older brother, he tries to present the image of a successful musician and gambler, but his music, his clothes and even his manner of presentation are old. He is a man who looking back over his life continues to live it with an odd mixture of zest and sorrow.)*

WINING BOY. So the Ghosts of the Yellow Dog got Sutter. That just go to show you I believe I always lived right. They say every dog gonna have his day and time it go around it sure come back to you. I done seen that a thousand times. I know the truth of that. But I'll tell you outright…if I see Sutter's ghost I'll be on the first thing I find that got wheels on it.

DOAKER. *(moving to the table)* Wining Boy!

WINING BOY. And I'll tell you another thing…Berniece ain't gonna sell that piano.

DOAKER. That's what she told him. He say he gonna cut it in half and go on and sell his half. They been around here three days trying to sell them watermelons. They trying to get out to where the white folks live but the truck keep breaking down. They go a block or two and it break down again. They trying to get out to Squirrel Hill and can't get around the corner. He say soon as he can get that truck empty to where he can set the piano up in there he gonna take it out of here and go sell it.

WINING BOY. What about them boys Sutter got? How come they ain't farming that land?

DOAKER. One of them going to school. He left down there and come North to school. The other one ain't got as much sense as that frying pan over yonder. That is the dumbest white man I ever seen. He'd stand in the river and watch it rise till it drown him.

WINING BOY. Other than seeing Sutter's ghost how's Berniece doing?

DOAKER. She doing all right. She still got Crawley on her mind. He been dead three years but she still holding on to him. She need to go out here and let one of these fellows grab a whole handful of whatever she got. She act like it done got precious.

WINING BOY. They always told me any fish will bite if you got good bait.

DOAKER. She stuck up on it. She think it's better than she is. I believe she messing around with Avery. They got something going. He a preacher now. If you let him tell it the Holy Ghost sat on his head and heaven opened up with thunder and lightning and God was calling his name. Told him to go out and preach and tend to his flock. That's what he gonna call his church. The Good Shepherd Church.

WINING BOY. They had that joker down in Spear walking around talking about he Jesus Christ. He gonna live the life of Christ. Went through the Last Supper and everything. Rented him a mule on Palm Sunday and rode through the town. Did everything...talking about he Christ. He did everything until they got up to that crucifixion part. Got up to that part and told everybody to go home and quit pretending. He got up to the crucifixion part and changed his mind. Had a whole bunch of folks come down there to see him get nailed to the cross. I don't know who's the worse fool. Him or them. Had all them folks come down there...even carried the cross up this little hill. People standing around waiting to see him get nailed to the cross and he stop everything and preach a little sermon and told everybody to go home. Had enough nerve to tell them to come to church on Easter Sunday to celebrate his resurrection.

DOAKER. I'm surprised Avery ain't thought about that. He trying every little thing to get him a congregation together. They meeting over at his house till he get him a church.

WINING BOY. Ain't nothing wrong with being a preacher. You got the preacher on one hand and the gambler on the other. Sometimes there ain't too much difference in them.

DOAKER. How long you been in Kansas City?

WINING BOY. Since I left here. I got tied up with some old gal down there. *(pause)* You know Cleotha died.

DOAKER. Yeah, I heard that last time I was down there. I was sorry to hear that.

WINING BOY. One of her friends wrote and told me. I got the letter right here. *(takes the letter out of his pocket)* I was down in Kansas City and she wrote and told me Cleotha had died. Name of Willa Bryant. She say she know Cousin Rupert. *(opens the letter and reads:)*

Dear Wining Boy

I am writing this letter to let you know Miss Cleotha Holman passed on Saturday the first of May she departed this world in the loving arms of her sister Miss Alberta Samuels. I know you would want to know this and am writing as a friend of Cleotha. There have been many hardships since last you seen her but she survived them all and to the end was a good woman whom I hope have God's Grace and is in his Paradise. Your cousin Rupert Bates is my friend also and he give me your address and I pray this reaches you about Cleotha.

Miss Willa Bryant,
A friend.

(He folds the letter and returns it to his pocket.)

They was nailing her coffin shut by the time I heard about it. I never knew she was sick. I believe it was that yellow jaundice. That's what killed her mama.

DOAKER. Cleotha wasn't but forty-some.

WINING BOY. She was forty-six. I got ten years on her. I met her when she was sixteen. You remember I used to run around there. Couldn't nothing keep me still. Much as I loved Cleotha I loved to ramble. Couldn't nothing keep me still. We got married and we used to fight about it all the time. Then one day she asked me to leave. Told me she loved me before I left. Told me, Wining Boy, you got a home as long as I got mine. And I believe in my heart I always felt that and that kept me safe.

DOAKER. Cleotha always did have a nice way about her.

WINING BOY. Man, that woman was something. I used to thank the Lord. Many a night I sat up and looked out over my life. Said, well, I had Cleotha. When it didn't look like there was nothing else for me, I said, thank God, at least I had that. If ever I go anywhere in this life I done known a good woman. And that used to hold me till the next morning. *(pause)* What you got? Give me a little nip. I know you got something stuck up in your room.

DOAKER. I ain't seen you walk in here and put nothing on the table. You done sat there and drank up your whiskey. Now you talking about what you got.

WINING BOY. I got plenty money. Give me a little nip.

> *(**DOAKER** carries a glass into his room and returns with it half-filled. He sets it on the table in front of **WINING BOY**.)*

You hear from Coreen?

DOAKER. She up in New York. I let her go from my mind.

WINING BOY. She was something back then. She wasn't too pretty but she had a way of looking at you made you know there was a whole lot of woman there. You got married and snatched her out from under us and we all got mad at you.

DOAKER. She up in New York City. That's what I hear.

(The door opens and **BOY WILLIE** *and* **LYMON** *enter.)*

BOY WILLIE. Aw hell...look here! We was just talking about you. Doaker say you left out of here with a whole sack of money. I told him we wasn't going see you till you got broke.

WINING BOY. What you mean broke? I got a whole pocketful of money.

DOAKER. Did you all get that truck fixed?

BOY WILLIE. We got it running and got halfway out there on Centre and it broke down again. Lymon went out there and messed it up some more. Fellow told us we got to wait till tomorrow to get it fixed. Say he have it running like new. Lymon going back down there and sleep in the truck so the people don't take the watermelons.

LYMON. Lymon nothing. You go down there and sleep in it.

BOY WILLIE. You was sleeping in it down home, nigger! I don't know nothing about sleeping in no truck.

LYMON. I ain't sleeping in no truck.

BOY WILLIE. They can take all the watermelons. I don't care. Wining Boy where you coming from? Where you been?

WINING BOY. I been down in Kansas City.

BOY WILLIE. You remember Lymon? Lymon Jackson.

WINING BOY. Yeah, I used to know his daddy.

BOY WILLIE. Doaker say you don't never leave no address with nobody. Say he got to depend on your whim. See when it strike you to pay a visit.

WINING BOY. I got four or five addresses.

BOY WILLIE. Doaker say Berniece asked you for three dollars and you got mad and left.

WINING BOY. Berniece try and rule over you too much for me. That's why I left. It wasn't about no three dollars.

BOY WILLIE. Where you getting all these sacks of money from? I need to be with you. Doaker say you had a whole sack of money...turn some of it loose.

WINING BOY. I was just fixing to ask you for five dollars.

BOY WILLIE. I ain't got no money. I'm trying to get some. Doaker tell you about Sutter? The Ghosts of the Yellow Dog got him about three weeks ago. Berniece done seen his ghost and everything. He right upstairs. *(calls)* Hey Sutter! Wining Boy's here. Come on, get a drink!

WINING BOY. How many that make the Ghosts of the Yellow Dog done got?

BOY WILLIE. Must be about nine or ten, eleven or twelve. I don't know

DOAKER. You got Ed Saunders. Howard Peterson. Charlie Webb.

WINING BOY. Robert Smith. That fellow that shot Becky's boy...say he was stealing peaches...

DOAKER. You talking about Bob Mallory.

BOY WILLIE. Berniece say she don't believe all that about the Ghosts of the Yellow Dog.

WINING BOY. She ain't got to believe. You go ask them white folks in Sunflower County if they believe. You go ask Sutter if he believe. I don't care if Berniece believe or not. I done been to where the Southern cross the Yellow Dog and called out their names. They talk back to you, too.

LYMON. What they sound like? The wind or something?

BOY WILLIE. You done been there for real, Wining Boy?

WINING BOY. Nineteen thirty. July of nineteen thirty I stood right there on that spot. It didn't look like nothing was going right in my life. I said everything can't go wrong all the time...let me go down there and call on the Ghosts of the Yellow Dog, see if they can help me. I went down there and right there where them two railroads cross each other...I stood right there on that spot and called out their names. They talk back to you, too.

LYMON. People say you can ask them questions. They talk to you like that?

WINING BOY. A lot of things you got to find out on your own. I can't say how they talked to nobody else. But to me it just filled me up in a strange sort of way to be standing there on that spot. I didn't want to leave. It felt like the longer I stood there the bigger I got. I seen the train coming and it seem like I was bigger than the train. I started not to move. But something told me to go ahead and get on out the way. The train passed and I started to go back up there and stand some more. But something told me not to do it. I walked away from there feeling like a king. Went on and had a stroke of luck that run on for three years. So I don't care if Berniece believe or not. Berniece ain't got to believe. I know 'cause I been there. Now Doaker'll tell you about the Ghosts of the Yellow Dog.

DOAKER. I don't try and talk that stuff with Berniece. Avery got her all tied up in that church. She just think it's a whole lot of nonsense.

BOY WILLIE. Berniece don't believe in nothing. She just think she believe. She believe in anything if it's convenient for her to believe. But when that convenience run out then she ain't got nothing to stand on.

WINING BOY. Let's not get on Berniece now. Doaker tell me you talking about selling that piano.

BOY WILLIE. Yeah...hey Doaker, I got the name of that man Avery was talking about. The man what's fixing the truck gave me his name. Everybody know him. Say he buy up anything you can make music with. I got his name and his telephone number. Hey Wining Boy Sutter's brother say he selling the land to me. I got one part. Sell them watermelons get me the second part. Then...soon as I get them watermelons out that truck I'm gonna take and sell that piano and get the third part.

DOAKER. That land ain't worth nothing no more. The smart white man's up here in these cities. He cut the land loose and step back and watch you and the dumb white man argue over it.

WINING BOY. How you know Sutter's brother ain't sold it already? You talking about selling the piano and the man's liable to sold the land two or three times.

BOY WILLIE. He say he waiting on me. He say he give me two weeks. That's two weeks from Friday. Say if I ain't back by then he might gonna sell it to somebody else. He say he wanna see me with it.

WINING BOY. You know as well as I know the man gonna sell the land to the first one walk up and hand him the money.

BOY WILLIE. That's just who I'm gonna be. Look, you ain't gotta know he waiting on me. I know. Okay. I know what the man told me. Stovall already done tried to buy the land from him and he told him no. The man say he waiting on me...he waiting on me. Hey Doaker...give me a drink. I see Wining Boy got his glass.

(**DOAKER** *exits into his room.*)

Wining Boy what you doing in Kansas City? What they got down there?

LYMON. I hear they got some nice-looking women in Kansas City. I sure like to go down there and find out.

WINING BOY. Man, the women down there is something else.

(**DOAKER** *enters with a bottle of whiskey. He sets it on the table with some glasses.*)

DOAKER. You wanna sit up here and drink up my whiskey, leave a dollar on the table when you get up.

BOY WILLIE. You ain't doing nothing but showing your hospitality. I know we ain't got to pay for your hospitality.

WINING BOY. Doaker say they had you and Lymon down on the Parchman Farm. Had you on my old stomping grounds.

BOY WILLIE. Me and Lymon was down there hauling wood for Jim Miller and keeping us a little bit to sell. Some white fellows tried to run us off of it. That's when Crawley got killed. They put me and Lymon in the penitentiary.

LYMON. They ambushed us right there where that road dip down and around that bend in the creek. Crawley tried to fight them. Me and Boy Willie got away but the sheriff got us. Say we was stealing wood. They shot me in my stomach.

BOY WILLIE. They looking for Lymon down there now. They rounded him up and put him in jail for not working.

LYMON. Fined me a hundred dollars. Mr. Stovall come and paid my hundred dollars and the judge say I got to work for him to pay him back his hundred dollars. I told them I'd rather take my thirty days but they wouldn't let me do that.

BOY WILLIE. As soon as Stovall turned his back, Lymon was gone. He down there living in that truck dodging the sheriff and Stovall. He got both of them looking for him. So I brought him up here.

LYMON. I told Boy Willie I'm gonna stay up here. I ain't going back with him.

BOY WILLIE. Ain't nobody twisting your arm to make you go back. You can do what you want to do.

WINING BOY. I'll go back with you. I'm on my way down there. You gonna take the train? I'm gonna take the train.

LYMON. They treat you better up here.

BOY WILLIE. I ain't worried about nobody mistreating me. They treat you like you let them treat you. They mistreat me I mistreat them right back. Ain't no difference in me and the white man.

WINING BOY. Ain't no difference as far as how somebody supposed to treat you. I agree with that. But I'll tell you the difference between the colored man and the white man. All right. Now you take and eat some berries. They taste real good to you. So you say I'm gonna go out and get me a whole pot of these berries and cook them up to make a pie or whatever. But you ain't looked to see them berries is sitting in the white fellow's yard. Ain't got no fence around them. You figure anybody want something they'd fence it in. All right. Now the white man come along and say that's my land. Therefore everything that grow on it belong to me. He tell the sheriff "I want you to put this nigger in jail as a warning to all the other niggers. Otherwise first thing you know these niggers have everything that belong to us."

BOY WILLIE. I'd come back at night and haul off his whole patch while he was sleep.

WINING BOY. All right. Now Mr. So and So, he sell the land to you. And he come to you and say, "John, you own the land. It's all yours now. But them is my berries. And come time to pick them I'm gonna send my boys over. You got the land...but them berries, I'm gonna keep them. They mine." And he go and fix it with the law that them is his berries. Now that's the difference between the colored man and the white man. The colored man can't fix nothing with the law.

BOY WILLIE. I don't go by what the law say. The law's liable to say anything. I go by if it's right or not. It don't matter to me what the law say. I take and look at it for myself.

LYMON. That's why you gonna end up back down there on the Parchman Farm.

BOY WILLIE. I ain't thinking about no Parchman Farm. You liable to go back before me.

LYMON. They work you too hard down there. All that weeding and hoeing and chopping down trees. I didn't like all that.

WINING BOY. You ain't got to like your job on Parchman. Hey, tell him, Doaker, the only one got to like his job is the water boy.

DOAKER. If he don't like his job he need to set that bucket down.

BOY WILLIE. That's what they told Lymon. They had Lymon on water and everybody got mad at him 'cause he was lazy.

LYMON. That water was heavy.

BOY WILLIE. They had Lymon down there singing. *(singing)*
O LORD BERTA BERTA O LORD GAL OH-AH
O LORD BERTA BERTA O LORD GAL WELL

(**LYMON** *and* **WINING BOY** *join in.*)

BOY WILLIE, LYMON AND WINING BOY. *(singing)*
GO 'HEAD MARRY DON'T YOU WAIT ON ME OH-AH
GO 'HEAD MARRY DON'T YOU WAIT ON ME WELL
MIGHT NOT WANT YOU WHEN I GO FREE OH-AH
MIGHT NOT WANT YOU WHEN I GO FREE WELL.

BOY WILLIE. Come on, Doaker. Doaker know this one.

(*As* **DOAKER** *joins in the men stamp and clap to keep time. They sing in harmony with great fervor and style.*)

BOY WILLIE, LYMON, WINING BOY AND DOAKER. *(singing)*
O LORD BERTA BERTA O LORD GAL OH-AH
O LORD BERTA BERTA O LORD GAL WELL

RAISE THEM UP HIGHER, LET THEM DROP ON DOWN OH-AH
RAISE THEM UP HIGHER, LET THEM DROP ON DOWN WELL
DON'T KNOW THE DIFFERENCE WHEN THE SUN GO DOWN
    OH-AH
DON'T KNOW THE DIFFERENCE WHEN THE SUN GO DOWN
    WELL

BERTA IN MERIDIAN AND SHE LIVING AT EASE OH-AH
BERTA IN MERIDIAN AND SHE LIVING AT EASE WELL
I'M ON OLD PARCHMAN, GOT TO WORK OR LEAVE OH-AH
I'M ON OLD PARCHMAN, GOT TO WORK OR LEAVE WELL

O ALBERTA, BERTA, O LORD GAL OH-AH
O ALBERTA, BERTA, O LORD GAL WELL

WHEN YOU MARRY, DON'T MARRY NO FARMING MAN OH-AH
WHEN YOU MARRY, DON'T MARRY NO FARMING MAN WELL
EVERY DAY MONDAY, HOE HANDLE IN YOUR HAND OH-AH
EVERY DAY MONDAY, HOE HANDLE IN YOUR HAND WELL

WHEN YOU MARRY, MARRY A RAILROAD MAN, OH-AH
WHEN YOU MARRY, MARRY A RAILROAD MAN, WELL
EVERY DAY SUNDAY, DOLLAR IN YOUR HAND OH-AH
EVERY DAY SUNDAY, DOLLAR IN YOUR HAND WELL

O ALBERTA, BERTA, O LORD GAL OH-AH
O ALBERTA, BERTA, O LORD GAL WELL.

BOY WILLIE. Doaker like that part. He like that railroad part.

LYMON. Doaker sound like Tangleye. He can't sing a lick.

BOY WILLIE. Hey, Doaker, they still talk about you down on Parchman. They ask me, "You Doaker Boy's nephew?" I say, "Yeah, me and him is family." They treated me all right soon as I told them that. Say, "Yeah, he my uncle."

DOAKER. I don't never want to see none of them niggers no more.

BOY WILLIE. I don't want to see them either. Hey, Wining Boy, come on play some piano. You a piano player, play some piano. Lymon wanna hear you.

WINING BOY. I give that piano up. That was the best thing that ever happened to me, getting rid of that piano. That piano got so big and I'm carrying it around on my back. I don't wish that on nobody. See, you think it's all fun being a recording star. Got to carrying that piano around and man did I get slow. Got just like molasses. The world just slipping by me and I'm walking around with that piano. All right. Now, there ain't but so many places you can go. Only so many road wide enough for you and that piano. And that piano get heavier and heavier. Go to a place and they find out you play piano, the first thing they want to do is give you a drink, find you a piano, and sit you right down. And that's where you gonna be for the next eight hours. They ain't gonna let you get up! Now, the first three or four years of that is fun. You can't get enough whiskey and you can't get enough women and you don't never get tired of playing that piano. But that only last so long. You look up one day and you hate the whiskey, and you hate the women, and you hate the piano. But that's all you got. You can't do nothing else. All you know how to do is play that piano. Now, who am I? Am I me? Or am I the piano player? Sometime it seem like the only thing to do is shoot the piano player 'cause he the cause of all the trouble I'm having.

DOAKER. What you gonna do when your troubles get like mine?

LYMON. If I knew how to play it, I'd play it. That's a nice piano.

BOY WILLIE. Whoever playing better play quick. Sutter's brother say he waiting on me. I sell them watermelons. Get Berniece to sell that piano. Put them two parts with the part I done saved...

WINING BOY. Berniece ain't gonna sell that piano. I don't see why you don't know that.

BOY WILLIE. What she gonna do with it? She ain't doing nothing but letting it sit up there and rot. That piano ain't doing nobody no good.

LYMON. That's a nice piano. If I had it I'd sell it. Unless I knew how to play like Wining Boy. You can get a nice price for that piano.

DOAKER. Now I'm gonna tell you something, Lymon don't know this...but I'm gonna tell you why me and Wining Boy say Berniece ain't gonna sell that piano.

BOY WILLIE. She ain't got to sell it! I'm gonna sell it! Berniece ain't got no more rights to that piano than I do.

DOAKER. I'm talking to the man...let me talk to the man. See, now...to understand why we say that... to understand about that piano...you got to go back to slavery time. See, our family was owned by a fellow named Robert Sutter. That was Sutter's grandfather. All right. The piano was owned by a fellow named Joel Nolander. He was one of the Nolander brothers from down in Georgia. It was coming up on Sutter's wedding anniversary and he was looking to buy his wife...Miss Ophelia was her name...he was looking to buy her an anniversary present. Only thing with him...he ain't had no money. But he had some niggers. So he asked Mr. Nolander to see if maybe he could trade off some of his niggers for that piano. Told him he would give him one-and-a-half niggers for it. That's the way he told him. Say he could have one full-grown and one half-grown. Mr. Nolander agreed only he say he had to pick them. He didn't want Sutter to give him just any old nigger. He say he wanted to have the pick of the litter. So Sutter lined up his niggers and Mr. Nolander looked them over and out of the whole bunch he picked my grandmother...her name was Berniece... same like Berniece...and he picked my daddy when he wasn't nothing but a little boy nine years old. They made the trade-off and Miss Ophelia was so happy with that piano that it got to be just about all she would do was play on that piano.

WINING BOY. Just get up in the morning, get all dressed up and sit down and play on that piano.

DOAKER. All right. Time go along. Time go along. Miss Ophelia got to missing my grandmother...the way she would cook and clean the house and talk to her and whatnot. And she missed having my daddy around the house to fetch things for her. So she asked to see if maybe she could trade back that piano and get her niggers back. Mr. Nolander said no. Said a deal was a deal. Him and Sutter had a big falling-out about it and Miss Ophelia took sick to the bed. Wouldn't get out of the bed in the morning. She just lay there. The doctor said she was wasting away.

WINING BOY. That's when Sutter called our granddaddy up to the house.

DOAKER. Now, our granddaddy's name was Boy Willie. That's who Boy Willie's named after…only they called him Willie Boy. Now, he was a worker of wood. He could make you anything you wanted out of wood. He'd make you a desk. A table. A lamp. Anything you wanted. Them white fellows around there used to come up to Mr. Sutter and get him to make all kinds of things for them. Then theyd pay Mr. Sutter a nice price. See, everything my granddaddy made Mr. Sutter owned 'cause he owned him. That's why when Mr. Nolander offered to buy him to keep the family together Mr. Sutter wouldn't sell him. Told Mr. Nolander he didn't have enough money to buy him. Now…am I telling it right, Wining Boy?

WINING BOY. You telling it.

DOAKER. Sutter called him up to the house and told him to carve my grandmother and my daddy's picture on the piano for Miss Ophelia. And he took and carved this…*(crosses to the piano)* See that right there? That's my grandmother, Berniece. She looked just like that. And he put a picture of my daddy when he wasn't nothing but a little boy the way he remembered him. He made them up out of his memory. Only thing…he didn't stop there. He carved all this. He got a picture of his mama…Mama Esther…and his daddy, Boy Charles.

WINING BOY. That was the first Boy Charles.

DOAKER. Then he put on the side here all kinds of things. See that? That's when him and Mama Berniece got married. They called it jumping the broom. That's how you got married in them days. Then he got here when my daddy was born…and here he got Mama Esther's funeral…and down here he got Mr. Nolander taking Mama Berniece and my daddy away down to his place in Georgia. He got all kinds of things what happened with our family. When Mr. Sutter seen the piano with all them carvings on it he got mad. He didn't ask for all that. But see...there wasn't nothing he could do about it. When Miss Ophelia seen it...she got excited. Now she had her piano and her niggers too. She took back to playing it and played on it right up till the day she died. All right...now see, our brother Boy Charles... that's Berniece and Boy Willie's daddy...he was the oldest of us three boys. He's dead now. But he would have been fifty-seven if he had lived. He died in 1911 when he was thirty-one years old. Boy Charles used to talk about that piano all the time. He never could get it off his mind. Two or three months go by and he be talking about it again. He be talking about taking it out of Sutter's house. Say it was the story of our whole family and as long as Sutter had it...he had us. Say we was still in slavery. Me and Wining Boy tried to talk him out of it but it wouldn't do any good. Soon as he quiet down about it he'd start up again. We seen where he wasn't gonna get it off his mind...so, on the Fourth of July, 1911...when Sutter was at the picnic what the county give every year...me and Wining Boy went on down there with him and took that piano out of Sutter's house. We put it on a wagon and me and Wining Boy carried it over into the next county with Mama Ola's people. Boy Charles decided to stay around there and wait until Sutter got home to make it look like business as usual.

Now, I don't know what happened when Sutter came home and found that piano gone. But somebody went up to Boy Charles's house and set it on fire. But he wasn't in there. He must have seen them coming 'cause he went down and caught the 3:57 Yellow Dog. He didn't know they was gonna come down and stop the train. Stopped the train and found Boy Charles in the boxcar with four of them hoboes. Must have got mad when they couldn't find the piano 'cause they set the boxcar afire and killed everybody. Now, nobody know who done that. Some people say it was Sutter 'cause it was his piano. Some people say it was Sheriff Carter.

Some people say it was Robert Smith and Ed Saunders. But don't nobody know for sure. It was about two months after that that Ed Saunders fell down his well. Just upped and fell down his well for no reason. People say it was the ghost of them men who burned up in the boxcar that pushed him in his well. They started calling them the Ghosts of the Yellow Dog. Now, that's how all that got started and that why we say Berniece ain't gonna sell that piano. 'Cause her daddy died over it.

BOY WILLIE. All that's in the past. If my daddy had seen where he could have traded that piano in for some land of his own, it wouldn't be sitting up here now. He spent his whole life farming on somebody else's land. I ain't gonna do that. See, he couldn't do no better. When he come along he ain't had nothing he could build on. His daddy ain't had nothing to give him. The only thing my daddy had to give me was that piano. And he died over giving me that. I ain't gonna let it sit up there and rot without trying to do something with it. If Berniece can't see that, then I'm gonna go ahead and sell my half. And you and Wining Boy know I'm right.

DOAKER. Ain't nobody said nothing about who's right and who's wrong. I was just telling the man about the piano. I was telling him why we say Berniece ain't gonna sell it.

LYMON. Yeah, I can see why you say that now. I told Boy Willie he ought to stay up here with me.

BOY WILLIE. You stay! I'm going back! That's what I'm gonna do with my life! Why I got to come up here and learn to do something I don't know how to do when I already know how to farm? You stay up here and make your own way if that's what you want to do. I'm going back and live my life the way I want to live it.

(**WINING BOY** *gets up and crosses to the piano.*)

WINING BOY. Let's see what we got here. I ain't played on this thing for a while.

DOAKER. You can stop telling that. You was playing on it the last time you was through here. We couldn't get you off of it. Go on and play something.

> (**WINING BOY** *sits down at the piano and plays and sings. The song is one which has put many dimes and quarters in his pocket, long ago, in dimly remembered towns and way stations. He plays badly, without hesitation, and sings in a forceful voice.*)

WINING BOY. *(singing)*
> I AM A RAMBLING GAMBLING MAN
> I GAMBLED IN MANY TOWNS
> I RAMBLED THIS WIDE WORLD OVER
> I RAMBLED THIS WORLD AROUND
> I HAD MY UPS AND DOWNS IN LIFE
> AND BITTER TIMES I SAW
> BUT I NEVER KNEW WHAT MISERY WAS
> TILL I LIT ON OLD ARKANSAS.
>
> I STARTED OUT ONE MORNING
> TO MEET THAT EARLY TRAIN
> HE SAID, "YOU BETTER WORK FOR ME
> I HAVE SOME LAND TO DRAIN.
> I'LL GIVE YOU FIFTY CENTS A DAY
> YOUR WASHING, BOARD AND ALL
> AND YOU SHALL BE A DIFFERENT MAN
> IN THE STATE OF ARKANSAS."
>
> I WORKED SIX MONTHS FOR THE RASCAL
> JOE HERRIN WAS HIS NAME
> HE FED ME OLD CORN DODGERS
> THEY WAS HARD AS ANY ROCK
> MY TOOTH IS ALL GOT LOOSENED
> AND MY KNEES BEGIN TO KNOCK
> THAT WAS THE KIND OF HASH I GOT
> IN THE STATE OF ARKANSAS.
>
> TRAVELING MAN
> I'VE TRAVELED ALL AROUND THIS WORLD
> TRAVELING MAN

I'VE TRAVELED FROM LAND TO LAND
TRAVELING MAN
I'VE TRAVELED ALL AROUND THIS WORLD
WELL IT AIN'T NO USE
WRITING NO NEWS
I'M A TRAVELING MAN.

(The door opens and **BERNIECE** *enters with* **MARETHA**.)

BERNIECE. Is that…Lord, I know that ain't Wining Boy sitting there.

WINING BOY. Hey, Berniece.

BERNIECE. You all had this planned. You and Boy Willie had this planned.

WINING BOY. I didn't know he was gonna be here. I'm on my way down home. I stopped by to see you and Doaker first.

DOAKER. I told the nigger he left out of here with that sack of money, we thought we might never see him again. Boy Willie say he wasn't gonna see him till he got broke. I looked up and seen him sitting on the doorstep asking for two dollars. Look at him laughing. He know it's the truth.

BERNIECE. Boy Willie, I didn't see that truck out there. I thought you was out selling watermelons.

BOY WILLIE. We done sold them all. Sold the truck too.

BERNIECE. I don't want to go through none of your stuff. I done told you to go back where you belong.

BOY WILLIE. I was just teasing you, woman. You can't take no teasing?

BERNIECE. Wining Boy, when you get here?

WINING BOY. A little while ago. I took the train from Kansas City.

BERNIECE. Let me go upstairs and change and then I'll cook you something to eat.

BOY WILLIE. You ain't cooked me nothing when I come.

BERNIECE. Boy Willie, go on and leave me alone. Come on, Maretha, get up here and change your clothes before you get them dirty.

> *(BERNIECE exits up the stairs, followed by MARETHA.)*

WINING BOY. Maretha sure getting big, ain't she, Doaker. And just as pretty as she want to be. I didn't know Crawley had it in him.

> *(BOY WILLIE crosses to the piano.)*

BOY WILLIE. Hey, Lymon...get up on the other side of this piano and let me see something.

WINING BOY. Boy Willie, what is you doing?

BOY WILLIE. I'm seeing how heavy this piano is. Get up over there, Lymon.

WINING BOY. Go on and leave that piano alone. You ain't taking that piano out of here and selling it.

BOY WILLIE. Just as soon as I get them watermelons out that truck.

WINING BOY. Well, I got something to say about that.

BOY WILLIE. This my daddy's piano.

WINING BOY. He ain't took it by himself. Me and Doaker helped him.

BOY WILLIE. He died by himself. Where was you and Doaker at then? Don't come telling me nothing about this piano. This is me and Berniece's piano. Am I right, Doaker?

DOAKER. Yeah, you right.

BOY WILLIE. Let's see if we can lift it up, Lymon. Get a good grip on it and pick it up on your end. Ready? Lift!

> *(As they start to move the piano, the sound of Sutter's Ghost is heard. DOAKER is the only one to hear it. With difficulty they move the piano a little bit so it is out of place.)*

What you think?

LYMON. It's heavy...but you can move it. Only it ain't gonna be easy.

BOY WILLIE. It wasn't that heavy to me. Okay let's put it back.

(The sound of Sutter's Ghost is heard again. They all hear it as BERNIECE *enters on the stairs.)*

BERNIECE. Boy Willie...you gonna play around with me one too many times. And then God's gonna bless you and West is gonna dress you. Now set that piano back over there. I done told you a hundred times I ain't selling that piano.

BOY WILLIE. I'm trying to get me some land, woman. I need that piano to get me some money so I can buy Sutter's land.

BERNIECE. Money can't buy what that piano cost. You can't sell your soul for money. It won't go with the buyer. It'll shrivel and shrink to know that you ain't taken on to it. But it won't go with the buyer.

BOY WILLIE. I ain't talking about all that, woman. I ain't talking about selling my soul. I'm talking about trading that piece of wood for some land. Get something under your feet. Land the only thing God ain't making no more of. You can always get you another piano. I'm talking about some land. What you get something out the ground from. That's what I'm talking about. You can't do nothing with that piano but sit up there and look at it.

BERNIECE. That's just what I'm gonna do. Wining Boy, you want me to fry you some pork chops?

BOY WILLIE. Now, I'm gonna tell you the way I see it. The only thing that make that piano worth something is them carvings Papa Willie Boy put on there. That's what make it worth something. That was my great-grandaddy. Papa Boy Charles brought that piano into the house. Now, I'm supposed to build on what they left me. You can't do nothing with that piano sitting up here in the house. That's just like if I let them watermelons sit out there and rot. I'd be a fool. All right now, if you say to me, Boy Willie, I'm using that piano. I give out lessons on it and that help me make my rent or whatever. Then that be something else. I'd have to go on and say, well, Berniece using that piano. She building on it. Let her go on and use it. I got to find another way to get Sutter's land. But Doaker say you ain't touched that piano the whole time it's been up here. So why you wanna stand in my way? See, you just looking at the sentimental value. See, that's good. That's all right. I take my hat off whenever somebody say my daddy's name. But I ain't gonna be no fool about no sentimental value. You can sit up here and look at the piano for the next hundred years and it's just gonna be a piano. You can't make more than that. Now I want to get Sutter's land with that piano. I get Sutter's land and I can go down and cash in the crop and get my seed. As long as I got the land and the seed then I'm all right. I can always get me a little something else. 'Cause that land give back to you. I can make me another crop and cash that in. I still got the land and the seed. But that piano don't put out nothing else. You ain't got nothing working for you. Now, the kind of man my daddy was he would have understood that. I'm sorry you can't see it that way. But that's why I'm gonna take that piano out of here and sell it.

BERNIECE. You ain't taking that piano out of my house. *(crosses to the piano)* Look at this piano. Look at it. Mama Ola polished this piano with her tears for seventeen years. For seventeen years she rubbed on it till her hands bled. Then she rubbed the blood in…mixed it up with the rest of the blood on it. Every day that God breathed life into her body she rubbed and cleaned and polished and prayed over it. "Play something for me, Berniece. Play something for me, Berniece." Every day. "I cleaned it up for you, play something for me, Berniece." You always talking about your daddy but you ain't never stopped to look at what his foolishness cost your mama. Seventeen years' worth of cold nights and an empty bed. For what? For a piano? For a piece of wood? To get even with somebody? I look at you and you're all the same. You, Papa Boy Charles, Wining Boy, Doaker, Crawley...you're all alike. All this thieving and killing and thieving and killing. And what it ever lead to? More killing and more thieving. I ain't never seen it come to nothing. People getting burned up. People getting shot. People falling down their wells. It don't never stop.

DOAKER. Come on now, Berniece, ain't no need in getting upset.

BOY WILLIE. I done a little bit of stealing here and there, but I ain't never killed nobody. I can't be speaking for nobody else. You all got to speak for yourself, but I ain't never killed nobody.

BERNIECE. You killed Crawley just as sure as if you pulled the trigger.

BOY WILLIE. See, that's ignorant. That's downright foolish for you to say something like that. You ain't doing nothing but showing your ignorance. If the nigger was here I'd whup his ass for getting me and Lymon shot at.

BERNIECE. Crawley ain't knew about the wood.

BOY WILLIE. We told the man about the wood. Ask Lymon. He knew all about the wood. He seen we was sneaking it. Why else we gonna be out there at night? Don't come telling me Crawley ain't knew about the wood. Them fellows come up on us and Crawley tried to bully them. Me and Lymon seen the sheriff with them and give in. Wasn't no sense in getting killed over fifty dollars' worth of wood.

BERNIECE. Crawley ain't knew you stole that wood.

BOY WILLIE. We ain't stole no wood. Me and Lymon was hauling wood for Jim Miller and keeping us a little bit on the side. We dumped our little bit down there by the creek till we had enough to make a load. Some fellows seen us and we figured we better get it before they did. We come up there and got Crawley to help us load it. Figured we'd cut him in. Crawley trying to keep the wolf from his door...we was trying to help him.

LYMON. Me and Boy Willie told him about the wood. We told him some fellows might be trying to beat us to it. He say let me go back and get my thirty-eight. That's what caused all the trouble.

BOY WILLIE. If Crawley ain't had the gun he'd be alive today.

LYMON. We had it about half loaded when they come up on us. We seen the sheriff with them and we tried to get away. We ducked around near the bend in the creek... but they was down there too. Boy Willie say let's give in. But Crawley pulled out his gun and started shooting. That's when they started shooting back.

BERNIECE. All I know is Crawley would be alive if you hadn't come up there and got him.

BOY WILLIE. I ain't had nothing to do with Crawley getting killed. That was his own fault.

BERNIECE. Crawley's dead and in the ground and you still walking around here eating. That's all I know. He went off to load some wood with you and ain't never come back.

BOY WILLIE. I told you, woman...I ain't had nothing to do with...

BERNIECE. He ain't here, is he? He ain't here! *(hits BOY WILLIE)* I said he ain't here. Is he?

> *(BERNIECE continues to hit BOY WILLIE, who doesn't move to defend himself, other than backing up and turning his head so that most of the blows fall on his chest and arms.)*

DOAKER. *(grabbing BERNIECE)* Come on, Berniece...let it go, it ain't his fault.

BERNIECE. He ain't here, is he? Is he?

BOY WILLIE. I told you I ain't responsible for Crawley.

BERNIECE. He ain't here.

BOY WILLIE. Come on now, Berniece...don't do this now. Doaker, get her. I ain't had nothing to do with Crawley...

BERNIECE. You come up there and got him!

BOY WILLIE. I done told you now. Doaker, get her. I ain't playing.

DOAKER. Come on. Berniece.

> (MARETHA *is heard screaming upstairs. It is a scream of stark terror.*)

MARETHA. *(offstage, calling)* Mama!...Mama!

> (*The lights fade to black.*)

ACT TWO

Scene One

(The lights come up on the kitchen. It is the following morning. **DOAKER** *is ironing the pants to his uniform. He has a pot cooking on the stove at the same time. He is singing a song. The song provides him with the rhythm for his work and he moves about the kitchen with the ease born of many years as a railroad cook.)*

DOAKER. *(singing)*
GONNA LEAVE JACKSON MISSISSIPPI
AND GO TO MEMPHIS
AND DOUBLE BACK TO JACKSON
COME ON DOWN TO HATTIESBURG
CHANGE CARS ON THE Y.D.
COMING THROUGH THE TERRITORY TO
MERIDIAN
AND MERIDIAN TO GREENVILLE
AND GREENVILLE TO MEMPHIS
I'M ON MY WAY AND I KNOW WHERE
CHANGE CARS ON THE KATY
LEAVING JACKSON
AND GOING THROUGH CLARKSDALE
HELLO WINONA!
COURTLAND!
BATESVILLE!
COMO!
SENATOBIA!
LEWISBURG!
SUNFLOWER!

GLENDORA!
SHARKEY!
AND DOUBLE BACK TO JACKSON
HELLO GREENWOOD
I'M ON MY WAY MEMPHIS
CLARKSDALE
MOORHEAD
INDIANOLA
CAN A HIGHBALL PASS THROUGH?
HIGHBALL ON THROUGH SIR
GRAND CARSON!
THIRTY-FIRST STREET DEPOT
FOURTH STREET DEPOT
MEMPHIS!

(**WINING BOY** *enters carrying a suit of clothes.*)

I thought you took that suit to the pawnshop?

WINING BOY. I went down there and the man tell me the suit is too old. Look at this suit. This is one hundred percent silk! How a silk suit gonna get too old? I know what it was he just didn't want to give me five dollars for it. Best he wanna give me is three dollars. I figure a silk suit is worth five dollars all over the world. I wasn't gonna part with it for no three dollars so I brought it back.

DOAKER. They got another pawnshop up on Wylie.

WINING BOY. I carried it up there. He say he don't take no clothes. Only thing he take is guns and radios. Maybe a guitar or two. Where's Berniece?

DOAKER. Berniece still at work. Boy Willie went down there to meet Lymon this morning. I guess they got that truck fixed, they been out there all day and ain't come back yet. Maretha scared to sleep up there now. Berniece don't know, but I seen Sutter before she did.

WINING BOY. Say what?

DOAKER. About three weeks ago. I had just come back from down there. Sutter couldn't have been dead more than three days. He was sitting over there at the piano. I come out to go to work…and he was sitting right there. Had his hand on top of his head just like Berniece said. I believe he broke his neck when he fell in the well. I kept quiet about it. I didn't see no reason to upset Berniece.

WINING BOY. Did he say anything? Did he say he was looking for Boy Willie?

DOAKER. He was just sitting there. He ain't said nothing. I went on out the door and left him sitting there. I figure as long as he was on the other side of the room everything be all right. I don't know what I would have done if he had started walking toward me.

WINING BOY. Berniece say he was calling Boy Willie's name.

DOAKER. I ain't heard him say nothing. He was just sitting there when I seen him. But I don't believe Boy Willie pushed him in the well. Sutter here 'cause of that piano. I heard him playing on it one time. I thought it was Berniece but then she don't play that kind of music. I come out here and ain't seen nobody but them piano keys was moving a mile a minute. Berniece need to go on and get rid of it. It ain't done nothing but cause trouble.

WINING BOY. I agree with Berniece. Boy Charles ain't took it to give it back. He took it 'cause he figure he had more right to it than Sutter did. If Sutter can't understand that…then that's just the way that go. Sutter dead and in the ground…don't care where his ghost is. He can hover around and play on the piano all he want. I want to see him carry it out the house. That's what I want to see. What time Berniece get home? I don't see how I let her get away from me this morning.

DOAKER. You up there sleep. Berniece leave out of here early in the morning. She out there in Squirrel Hill cleaning house for some big shot down there at the steel mill. They don't like you to come late. You come late they won't give you your carfare. What kind of business you got with Berniece?

WINING BOY. My business. I ain't asked you what kind of business you got.

DOAKER. Berniece ain't got no money. If that's why you was trying to catch her. She having a hard enough time trying to get by as it is. If she go ahead and marry Avery...he working every day...she go ahead and marry him they could do all right for themselves. But as it stands she ain't got no money.

WINING BOY. Well, let me have five dollars.

DOAKER. I just give you a dollar before you left out of here. You ain't gonna take my five dollars out there and gamble and drink it up.

WINING BOY. Aw, nigger, give me five dollars. I'll give it back to you.

DOAKER. You wasn't looking to give me five dollars when you had that sack of money. You wasn't looking to throw nothing my way. Now you wanna come in here and borrow five dollars. If you going back with Boy Willie you need to be trying to figure out how you gonna get train fare.

WINING BOY. That's why I need the five dollars. If I had five dollars I could get me some money.

> (**DOAKER** *goes into his pocket.*)

Make it seven.

DOAKER. You take this five dollars...and you bring my money back here too.

> (**BOY WILLIE** *and* **LYMON** *enter. They are happy and excited. They have money in all of their pockets and are anxious to count it.*)

Howd you do out there?

BOY WILLIE. They was lining up for them.

LYMON. Me and Boy Willie couldn't sell them fast enough. Time we got one sold we'd sell another.

BOY WILLIE. I seen what was happening and told lymon to up the price on them.

LYMON. Boy Willie say charge them a quarter more. They didn't care. A couple of people give me a dollar and told me to keep the change.

BOY WILLIE. One fellow bought five. I say now what he gonna do with five watermelons? He can't eat them all. I sold him the five and asked him did he want to buy five more.

LYMON. I ain't never seen nobody snatch a dollar fast as Boy Willie.

BOY WILLIE. One lady asked me say, "Is they sweet?" I told her say, "Lady, where we grow these watermelons we put sugar in the ground." You know, she believed me. Talking about she had never heard of that before. Lymon was laughing his head off. I told her, "Oh, yeah, we put the sugar right in the ground with the seed." She say, "Well, give me another one." Them white folks is something else...ain't they, Lymon?

LYMON. Soon as you holler watermelons they come right out their door. Then they go and get their neighbors. Look like they having a contest to see who can buy the most.

WINING BOY. I got something for Lymon.

> (**WINING BOY** *gets his suit.* **BOY WILLIE** *and* **LYMON** *continue to count their money.*)

BOY WILLIE. I know you got more than that. You ain't sold all them watermelons for that little bit of money.

LYMON. I'm still looking. That ain't all you got either. Where's all them quarters?

BOY WILLIE. You let me worry about the quarters. Just put the money on the table.

WINING BOY. *(entering with his suit)* Look here, Lymon...see this? Look at his eyes getting big. He ain't never seen a suit like this. This is one hundred percent silk. Go ahead...put it on. See if it fit you.

> (**LYMON** *tries the suit coat on.*)

Look at that. Feel it. That's one hundred percent genuine silk. I got that in Chicago. You can't get clothes like that nowhere but New York and Chicago. You can't get clothes like that in Pittsburgh. These folks in Pittsburgh ain't never seen clothes like that.

LYMON. This is nice, feel real nice and smooth.

WINING BOY. That's a fifty-five-dollar suit. That's the kind of suit the big shots wear. You need a pistol and a pocketful of money to wear that suit. I'll let you have it for three dollars. The women will fall out their windows they see you in a suit like that. Give me three dollars and go on and wear it down the street and get you a woman.

BOY WILLIE. That looks nice, Lymon. Put the pants on. Let me see it with the pants.

(LYMON *begins to try on the pants.*)

WINING BOY. Look at that...see how it fits you? Give me three dollars and go on and take it. Look at that, Doaker...don't he look nice?

DOAKER. Yeah...that's a nice suit.

WINING BOY. Got a shirt to go with it. Cost you an extra dollar. Four dollars you got the whole deal.

LYMON. How this look, Boy Willie?

BOY WILLIE. That look nice...if you like that kind of thing. I don't like them dress-up kind of clothes. If you like it, look real nice.

WINING BOY. That's the kind of suit you need for up here in the North.

LYMON. Four dollars for everything? The suit and the shirt?

WINING BOY. That's cheap. I should be charging you twenty dollars. I give you a break 'cause you a homeboy. That's the only way I let you have it for four dollars.

LYMON. *(going into his pocket)* Okay...here go the four dollars.

WINING BOY. You got some shoes? What size you wear?

LYMON. Size nine.

WINING BOY. That's what size I got! Size nine. I let you have them for three dollars.

LYMON. Where they at? Let me see them.

WINING BOY. They real nice shoes, too. Got a nice tip to them. Got pointy toe just like you want.

(**WINING BOY** *goes to get his shoes.*)

LYMON. Come on, Boy Willie, let's go out tonight. I wanna see what it looks like up here. Maybe we go to a picture show. Hey, Doaker, they got picture shows up here?

DOAKER. The Rhumba Theater. Right down there on Fullerton Street. Can't miss it. Got the speakers outside on the sidewalk. You can hear it a block away. Boy Willie know where it's at.

(**DOAKER** *exits into his room.*)

LYMON. Let's go to the picture show, Boy Willie. Let's go find some women.

BOY WILLIE. Hey, Lymon, how many of them watermelons would you say we got left? We got just under a half a load...right?

LYMON. About that much. Maybe a little more.

BOY WILLIE. You think that piano will fit up in there?

LYMON. If we stack them watermelons you can sit it up in the front there.

BOY WILLIE. I'm gonna call that man tomorrow.

WINING BOY. *(returns with his shoes)* Here you go...size nine. Put them on. Cost you three dollars. That's a Florsheim shoe. That's the kind Stagger Lee wore.

LYMON. *(trying on the shoes)* You sure these size nine?

WINING BOY. You can look at my feet and see we wear the same size. Man, you put on that suit and them shoes and you got something there. You ready for whatever's out there. But is they ready for you? With them shoes on you be the King of the Walk. Have everybody stop to look at your shoes. Wishing they had a pair. I'll give you a break. Go on and take them for two dollars.

(**LYMON** *pays* **WINING BOY** *two dollars.*)

LYMON. Come on, Boy Willie…let's go find some women. I'm gonna go upstairs and get ready. I'll be ready to go in a minute. Ain't you gonna get dressed?

BOY WILLIE. I'm gonna wear what I got on. I ain't dressing up for these city niggers.

(**LYMON** *exits up the stairs.*)

That's all Lymon think about is women.

WINING BOY. His daddy was the same way. I used to run around with him. I know his mama too. Two strokes back and I would have been his daddy! His daddy's dead now…but I got the nigger out of jail one time. They was fixing to name him Daniel and walk him through the Lion's Den. He got in a tussle with one of them white fellows and the sheriff lit on him like white on rice. That's how the whole thing come about between me and Lymon's mama. She knew me and his daddy used to run together and he got in jail and she went down there and took the sheriff a hundred dollars. Don't get me to lying about where she got it from. I don't know. The sheriff looked at that hundred dollars and turned his nose up. Told her say, "That ain't gonna do him no good. You got to put another hundred on top of that." She come up there and got me where I was playing at this saloon…said she had all but fifty dollars and asked me if I could help. Now the way I figured it…without that fifty dollars the sheriff was gonna turn him over to Parchman. The sheriff turn him over to Parchman it be three years before anybody see him again. Now I'm gonna say it right…I will give anybody fifty dollars to keep them out of jail for three years. I give her the fifty dollars and she told me to come over to the house. I ain't asked her. I figure if she was nice enough to invite me I ought to go. I ain't had to say a word. She invited me over just as nice. Say "Why don't you come over to the house?" She ain't had to say nothing else. Them words rolled off her tongue just as nice. I went on down there and sat about three hours. Started to leave and changed my mind. She grabbed hold to me and say, "Baby, it's all night long." That was one of the shortest nights I have ever spent on this earth! I could have used another eight hours. Lymon's daddy didn't even say nothing to me when he got out. He just looked at me funny. He had a good notion something had happened between me an' her. L. D. Jackson. That was one bad-luck nigger. Got killed at some dance. Fellow walked in and shot him thinking he was somebody else.

(DOAKER *enters from his room.*)

Hey, Doaker, you remember L. D. Jackson?

DOAKER. That's Lymon's daddy. That was one bad-luck nigger.

BOY WILLIE. Look like you ready to railroad some.

DOAKER. Yeah, I got to make that run.

(LYMON *enters from the stairs. He is dressed in his new suit and shoes, to which he has added a cheap straw hat.*)

LYMON. How I look?

WINING BOY. You look like a million dollars. Don't he look good, Doaker? Come on, let's play some cards. You wanna play some cards?

BOY WILLIE. We ain't gonna play no cards with you. Me and Lymon gonna find some women. Hey, Lymon, don't play no cards with Wining Boy. He'll take all your money.

WINING BOY. *(to* LYMON*)* You got a magic suit there. You can get you a woman easy with that suit...but you got to know the magic words. You know the magic words to get you a woman?

LYMON. I just talk to them to see if I like them and they like me.

WINING BOY. You just walk right up to them and say, "If you got the harbor I got the ship." If that don't work ask them if you can put them in your pocket. The first thing they gonna say is, "It's too small." That's when you look them dead in the eye and say, "Baby, ain't nothing small about me." If that don't work then you move on to another one. Am I telling him right, Doaker?

DOAKER. That man don't need you to tell him nothing about no women. These women these days ain't gonna fall for that kind of stuff. You got to buy them a present. That's what they looking for these days.

BOY WILLIE. Come on, I'm ready. You ready Lymon? Come on, let's go find some women.

WINING BOY. Here, let me walk out with you. I wanna see the women fall out their window when they see Lymon.

(They all exit as the lights go down on the scene.)

Scene Two

(The lights come up on the kitchen. It is late evening of the same day. BERNIECE has set a tub for her bath in the kitchen. She is heating up water on the stove. There is a knock at the door.)

BERNIECE. Who is it?

AVERY. It's me, Avery.

(BERNIECE opens the door and lets him in.)

BERNIECE. Avery, come on in. I was just fixing to take my bath.

AVERY. Where Boy Willie? I see that truck out there almost empty. They done sold almost all them watermelons.

BERNIECE. They was gone when I come home. I don't know where they went off to. Boy Willie around here about to drive me crazy.

AVERY. They sell them watermelons...he'll be gone soon.

BERNIECE. What Mr. Cohen say about letting you have the place?

AVERY. He say he'll let me have it for thirty dollars a month. I talked him out of thirty-five and he say he'll let me have it for thirty.

BERNIECE. That's a nice spot next to Benny Diamond's store.

AVERY. Berniece...I be at home and I get to thinking you up here an' I'm down there. I get to thinking how that look to have a preacher that ain't married. It makes for a better congregation if the preacher was settled down and married.

BERNIECE. Avery...not now. I was fixing to take my bath.

AVERY. You know how I feel about you, Berniece. Now...I done got the place from Mr. Cohen. I get the money from the bank and I can fix it up real nice. They give me a ten-cents-a-hour raise down there on the job... now Berniece, I ain't got much in the way of comforts. I got a hole in my pockets near about as far as money is

concerned. I ain't never found no way through life to a
woman I care about like I care about you. I need that. I
need somebody on my bond side. I need a woman that
fits in my hand.

BERNIECE. Avery, I ain't ready to get married now.

AVERY. You too young a woman to close up, Berniece.

BERNIECE. I ain't said nothing about closing up. I got a lot
of woman left in me.

AVERY. Where's it at? When's the last time you looked at it?

BERNIECE. *(stunned by his remark)* That's a nasty thing to say.
And you call yourself a preacher.

AVERY. Any time I get anywhere near you...you push me
away.

BERNIECE. I got enough on my hands with Maretha. I got
enough people to love and take care of.

AVERY. Who you got to love you? Can't nobody get close
enough to you. Doaker can't half say nothing to you.
You jump all over Boy Willie. Who you got to love you,
Berniece?

BERNIECE. You trying to tell me a woman can't be nothing
without a man. But you all right, huh? You can just walk
out of here without me – without a woman – and still
be a man. That's all right. Ain't nobody gonna ask you,
"Avery, who you got to love you?" That's all right for
you. But everybody gonna be worried about Berniece.
"How Berniece gonna take care of herself? How she
gonna raise that child without a man? Wonder what
she do with herself How she gonna live like that?"
Everybody got all kinds of questions for Berniece.
Everybody telling me I can't be a woman unless I got a
man. Well, you tell me, Avery – you know – how much
woman am I?

AVERY. It wasn't me, Berniece. You can't blame me for
nobody else. I'll own up to my own shortcomings. But
you can't blame me for Crawley or nobody else.

BERNIECE. I ain't blaming nobody for nothing. I'm just
stating the facts.

AVERY. How long you gonna carry Crawley with you, Berniece? It's been over three years. At some point you got to let go and go on. Life's got all kinds of twists and turns. That don't mean you stop living. That don't mean you cut yourself off from life. You can't go through life carrying Crawley's ghost with you. Crawley's been dead three years. Three years, Berniece.

BERNIECE. I know how long Crawley's been dead. You ain't got to tell me that. I just ain't ready to get married right now.

AVERY. What is you ready for, Berniece? You just gonna drift along from day to day. Life is more than making it from one day to another. You gonna look up one day and it's all gonna be past you. Life's gonna be gone out of your hands – there won't be enough to make nothing with. I'm standing here now, Berniece – but I don't know how much longer I'm gonna be standing here waiting on you.

BERNIECE. Avery, I told you…when you get your church we'll sit down and talk about this. I got too many other things to deal with right now. Boy Willie and the piano…and Sutter's ghost. I thought I might have been seeing things, but Maretha done seen Sutter's ghost, too.

AVERY. When this happen, Berniece?

BERNIECE. Right after I came home yesterday. Me and Boy Willie was arguing about the piano and Sutter's ghost was standing at the top of the stairs. Maretha scared to sleep up there now. Maybe if you bless the house he'll go away.

AVERY. I don't know, Berniece. I don't know if I should fool around with something like that.

BERNIECE. I can't have Maretha scared to go to sleep up there. Seem like if you bless the house he would go away.

AVERY. You might have to be a special kind of preacher to do something like that.

BERNIECE. I keep telling myself when Boy Willie leave he'll go on and leave with him. I believe Boy Willie pushed him in the well.

AVERY. That's been going on down there a long time. The Ghosts of the Yellow Dog been pushing people in their wells long before Boy Willie got grown.

BERNIECE. Somebody down there pushing them people in their wells. They ain't just upped and fell. Ain't no wind pushed nobody in their well.

AVERY. Oh, I don't know. God works in mysterious ways.

BERNIECE. He ain't pushed nobody in their wells.

AVERY. He caused it to happen. God is the Great Causer. He can do anything. He parted the Red Sea. He say, "I will smite my enemies." Reverend Thompson used to preach on the Ghosts of the Yellow Dog as the hand of God.

BERNIECE. I don't care who preached what. Somebody down there pushing them people in their wells. Somebody like Boy Willie. I can see him doing something like that. You ain't gonna tell me that Sutter just upped and fell in his well. I believe Boy Willie pushed him so he could get his land.

AVERY. What Doaker say about Boy Willie selling the piano?

BERNIECE. Doaker don't want no part of that piano. He ain't never wanted no part of it. He blames himself for not staying behind with Papa Boy Charles. He washed his hands of that piano a long time ago. He didn't want me to bring it up here – but I wasn't gonna leave it down there.

AVERY. Well, it seems to me somebody ought to be able to talk to Boy Willie.

BERNIECE. You can't talk to Boy Willie. He been that way all his life. Mama Ola had her hands full trying to talk to him. He don't listen to nobody. He just like my daddy. He get his mind fixed on something and can't nobody turn him from it.

AVERY. You ought to start a choir at the church. Maybe if he seen you was doing something with it – if you told him you was gonna put it in my church – maybe he'd see it different. You ought to put it down in the church and start a choir. The Bible say "Make a joyful noise unto the Lord." Maybe if Boy Willie see you was doing something with it he'd see it different.

BERNIECE. I done told you I don't play on that piano. Ain't no need in you to keep talking this choir stuff. When my mama died I shut the top on that piano and I ain't never opened it since. I was only playing it for her. When my daddy died seem like all her life went into that piano. She used to have me playing on it…had Miss Eula come in and teach me…say when I played it she could hear my daddy talking to her. I used to think them pictures came alive and walked through the house. Sometime late at night I could hear my mama talking to them. I said that wasn't gonna happen to me. I don't play that piano 'cause I don't want to wake them spirits. They never be walking around in this house.

AVERY. You got to put all that behind you, Berniece.

BERNIECE. I got Maretha playing on it. She don't know nothing about it. Let her go on and be a schoolteacher or something. She don't have to carry all of that with her. She got a chance I didn't have. I ain't gonna burden her with that piano.

AVERY. You got to put all of that behind you, Berniece. That's the same thing like Crawley. Everybody got stones in their passway. You got to step over them or walk around them. You picking them up and carrying them with you. All you got to do is set them down by the side of the road. You ain't got to carry them with you. You can walk over there right now and play that piano. You can walk over there right now and God will walk over there with you. Right now you can set that sack of stones down by the side of the road and walk away from it. You don't have to carry it with you. You can do it right now. *(crosses over to the piano and raises the lid)*

Come on, Berniece…set it down and walk away from it. Come on, play "Old Ship of Zion." Walk over here and claim it as an instrument of the Lord. You can walk over here right now and make it into a celebration.

(**BERNIECE** *moves toward the piano.*)

BERNIECE. Avery…I done told you I don't want to play that piano. Now or no other time.

AVERY. The Bible say, "The Lord is my refuge…and my strength!" With the strength of God you can put the past behind you, Berniece. With the strength of God you can do anything! God got a bright tomorrow. God don't ask what you done…God ask what you gonna do. The strength of God can move mountains! God's got a bright tomorrow for you…all you got to do is walk over here and claim it.

BERNIECE. Avery, just go on and let me finish my bath. I'll see you tomorrow.

AVERY. Okay, Berniece. I'm gonna go home. I'm gonna go home and read up on my Bible. And tomorrow…if the good Lord give me strength tomorrow…I'm gonna come by and bless the house…and show you the power of the Lord. *(crosses to the door)* It's gonna be all right, Berniece. God say he will soothe the troubled waters. I'll come by tomorrow and bless the house.

(*The lights fade to black.*)

Scene Three

*(Several hours later. The house is dark. **BERNIECE** has retired for the night. **BOY WILLIE** enters the darkened house with **GRACE**.)*

BOY WILLIE. Come on in. This my sister's house. My sister live here. Come on, I ain't gonna bite you.

GRACE. Put some light on. I can't see.

BOY WILLIE. You don't need to see nothing, baby. This here is all you need to see. All you need to do is see me. If you can't see me you can feel me in the dark. How's that, sugar?

(He attempts to kiss her.)

GRACE. Go on now…wait!

BOY WILLIE. Just give me one little old kiss.

GRACE. *(pushing him away)* Come on, now. Where I'm gonna sleep at?

BOY WILLIE. We got to sleep out here on the couch. Come on, my sister don't mind. Lymon come back he just got to sleep on the floor. He run off with Dolly somewhere he better stay there. Come on, sugar.

GRACE. Wait now…you ain't told me nothing about no couch. I thought you had a bed. Both of us can't sleep on that little old couch.

BOY WILLIE. It don't make no difference. We can sleep on the floor. Let Lymon sleep on the couch.

GRACE. You ain't told me nothing about no couch.

BOY WILLIE. What difference it make? You just wanna be with me.

GRACE. I don't want to be with you on no couch. Ain't you got no bed?

BOY WILLIE. You don't need no bed, woman. My granddaddy used to take women on the backs of horses. What you need a bed for? You just want to be with me.

GRACE. You sure is country. I didn't know you was this country.

BOY WILLIE. There's a lot of things you don't know about me. Come on, let me show you what this country boy can do.

GRACE. Let's go to my place. I got a room with a bed if Leroy don't come back there.

BOY WILLIE. Who's Leroy? You ain't said nothing about no Leroy.

GRACE. He used to be my man. He ain't coming back. He gone off with some other gal.

BOY WILLIE. You let him have your key?

GRACE. He ain't coming back.

BOY WILLIE. Did you let him have your key?

GRACE. He got a key but he ain't coming back. He took off with some other gal.

BOY WILLIE. I don't wanna go nowhere he might come. Let's stay here. Come on, sugar. *(pulls her over to the couch)* Let me heist your hood and check your oil. See if your battery needs charged.

> *(He pulls her to him. They kiss and tug at each other's clothing. In their anxiety they knock over a lamp.)*

BERNIECE. *(offstage, yelling)* Who's that...Wining Boy?

BOY WILLIE. It's me...Boy Willie. Go on back to sleep. Everything's all right. *(to GRACE)* That's my sister. Everything's all right, Berniece. Go on back to sleep.

BERNIECE. *(offstage)* What you doing down there? What you done knocked over?

BOY WILLIE. It wasn't nothing. Everything's all right. Go on back to sleep. *(to GRACE)* That's my sister. We all right. She gone back to sleep.

> *(They begin to kiss. BERNIECE enters from the stairs dressed in a nightgown. She cuts on the light.)*

BERNIECE. Boy Willie, what you doing down here?

BOY WILLIE. It was just that there lamp. It ain't broke. It's okay. Everything's all right. Go on back to bed.

BERNIECE. Boy Willie, I don't allow that in my house. You gonna have to take your company someplace else.

BOY WILLIE. It's all right. We ain't doing nothing. We just sitting here talking. This here is Grace. That's my sister Berniece.

BERNIECE. You know I don't allow that kind of stuff in my house.

BOY WILLIE. Allow what? We just sitting here talking.

BERNIECE. Well, your company gonna have to leave. Come back and talk in the morning.

BOY WILLIE. Go on back upstairs now.

BERNIECE. I got an eleven-year-old girl upstairs. I can't allow that around here.

BOY WILLIE. Ain't nobody said nothing about that. I told you we just talking.

GRACE. Come on...let's go to my place. Ain't nobody got to tell me to leave but once.

BOY WILLIE. You ain't got to be like that, Berniece.

BERNIECE. I'm sorry, miss. But he know I don't allow that in here.

GRACE. You ain't got to tell me but once. I don't stay nowhere I ain't wanted.

BOY WILLIE. I don't know why you want to embarrass me in front of my company.

GRACE. Come on, take me home.

BERNIECE. Go on, Boy Willie. Just go on with your company.

> (**BOY WILLIE** *and* **GRACE** *exit.* **BERNIECE** *puts the light on in the kitchen and puts on the teakettle. There is a knock at the door.* **BERNIECE** *goes to answer it. She opens the door.* **LYMON** *enters.*)

LYMON. How you doing, Berniece? I thought you'd be asleep. Boy Willie been back here?

BERNIECE. He just left out of here a minute ago.

LYMON. I went out to see a picture show and never got there. We always end up doing something else. I was with this woman she just wanted to drink up all my money. So I left her there and came back looking for Boy Willie.

BERNIECE. You just missed him. He just left out of here.

LYMON. They got some nice-looking women in this city. I'm gonna like it up here real good. I like seeing them with their dresses on. Got them high heels. I like that. Make them look like they real precious. Boy Willie met a real nice one today. I wish I had met her before he did.

BERNIECE. He come by here with some woman a little while ago. I told him to go on and take all that out of my house.

LYMON. What she look like, the woman he was with? Was she a brown-skinned woman about this high? Nice and healthy? Got nice hips on her?

BERNIECE. She had on a red dress.

LYMON. That's her! That's Grace. She real nice. Laugh a lot. Lot of fun to be with. She don't be trying to put on. Some of these woman act like they the Queen of Sheba. I don't like them kind. Grace ain't like that. She real nice with herself.

BERNIECE. I don't know what she was like. He come in here all drunk knocking over the lamp, and making all kind of noise. I told them to take that somewhere else. I can't really say what she was like.

LYMON. She real nice. I seen her before he did. I was trying not to act like I seen her. I wanted to look at her a while before I said something. She seen me when I come into the saloon. I tried to act like I didn't see her. Time I looked around Boy Willie was talking to her. She was talking to him kept looking at me. That's when her friend Dolly came. I asked her if she wanted to go to the picture show. She told me to buy her a drink while she thought about it. Next thing I knew she done had three drinks talking about she too tired to go. I bought her another drink, then I left. Boy Willie was gone and I thought he might have come back here. Doaker gone, huh? He say he had to make a trip.

BERNIECE. Yeah, he gone on his trip. This is when I can usually get me some peace and quiet, Maretha asleep.

LYMON. She look just like you. Got them big eyes. I remember her when she was in diapers.

BERNIECE. Time just keep on. It go on with or without you. She going on twelve.

LYMON. She sure is pretty. I like kids.

BERNIECE. Boy Willie say you staying…what you gonna do up here in this big city? You thought about that?

LYMON. They never get me back down there. The sheriff looking for me. All because they gonna try and make me work for somebody when I don't want to. They gonna try and make me work for Stovall when he don't pay nothing. It ain't like that up here. Up here you more or less do what you want to. I figure I find me a job and try to get set up and then see what the year brings. I tried to do that two or three times down there…but it never would work out. I was always in the wrong place.

BERNIECE. This ain't a bad city once you get to know your way around.

LYMON. Up here is different. I'm gonna get me a job unloading boxcars or something. One fellow told me say he know a place. I'm gonna go over there with him next week. Me and Boy Willie finish selling them watermelons I'll have enough money to hold me for a while. But I'm gonna go over there and see what kind of jobs they have.

BERNIECE. You shouldn't have too much trouble finding a job. It's all in how you present yourself. See now, Boy Willie couldn't get no job up here. Somebody hire him they got a pack of trouble on their hands. Soon as they find that out they fire him. He don't want to do nothing unless he do it his way.

LYMON. I know. I told him let's go to the picture show first and see if there was any women down there. They might get tired of sitting at home and walk down to the picture show. He say he wanna look around first. We never did get down there. We tried a couple of places and then we went to this saloon where he met Grace. I tried to meet her before he did but he beat me to her. We left Wining Boy sitting down there running his mouth. He told me if I wear this suit I'd find me a woman. He was almost right.

BERNIECE. You don't need to be out there in them saloons. Ain't no telling what you liable to run into out there. This one liable to cut you as quick as that one shoot you. You don't need to be out there. You start out that fast life you can't keep it up. It makes you old quick. I don't know what them women out there be thinking about.

LYMON. Mostly they be lonely and looking for somebody to spend the night with them. Sometimes it matters who it is and sometimes it don't. I used to be the same way. Now it got to matter. That's why I'm here now. Dolly liable not to even recognize me if she sees me again. I don't like women like that. I like my women to be with me in a nice and easy way. That way we can both enjoy ourselves. The way I see it we the only two people like us in the world. We got to see how we fit together. A woman that don't want to take the time to do that I don't bother with. Used to. Used to bother with all of them. Then I woke up one time with this woman and I didn't know who she was. She was the prettiest woman I had ever seen in my life. I spent the whole night with her and didn't even know it. I had never taken the time to look at her. I guess she kinda knew I ain't never really looked at her. She must have known that cause she ain't wanted to see me no more. If she had wanted to see me I believe we might have got married. How come you ain't married? It seem like to me you would be married. I remember Avery from down home. I used to call him plain old Avery. Now he Reverend Avery. That's kinda funny about him becoming a preacher. I like when he told about how that come to him in a dream about them sheep people and them hoboes. Nothing ever come to me in a dream like that. I just dream about women. Can't never seem to find the right one.

BERNIECE. She out there somewhere. You just got to get yourself ready to meet her. That's what I'm trying to do. Avery's all right. I ain't really got nobody in mind.

LYMON. I get me a job and a little place and get set up to where I can make a woman comfortable I might get married. Avery's nice. You ought to go ahead and get married. You be a preacher's wife you won't have to work. I hate living by myself. I didn't want to be no strain on my mama so I left home when I was about sixteen. Everything I tried seem like it just didn't work out. Now I'm trying this.

BERNIECE. You keep trying it'll work out for you.

LYMON. You ever go down there to the picture show?

BERNIECE. I don't go in for all that.

LYMON. Ain't nothing wrong with it. It ain't like gambling and sinning. I went to one down in Jackson once. It was fun.

BERNIECE. I just stay home most of the time. Take care of Maretha.

LYMON. It's getting kind of late. I don't know where Boy Willie went off to. He's liable not to come back. I'm gonna take off these shoes. My feet hurt. Was you in bed? I don't mean to be keeping you up.

BERNIECE. You ain't keeping me up. I couldn't sleep after that Boy Willie woke me up.

LYMON. You got on that nightgown. I likes women when they wear them fancy nightclothes and all. It makes their skin look real pretty.

BERNIECE. I got this at the five-and-ten-cents store. It ain't so fancy.

LYMON. I don't too often get to see a woman dressed like that.

> *(There is a long pause.* **LYMON** *takes off his suit coat.)*

Well, I'm gonna sleep here on the couch. I'm supposed to sleep on the floor but I don't reckon Boy Willie's coming back tonight. Wining Boy sold me this suit. Told me it was a magic suit. I'm gonna put it on again tomorrow. Maybe it bring me a woman like he say. *(goes into his coat pocket and takes out a small bottle of perfume)* I almost forgot I had this. Some man sold me this for a dollar. Say it come from Paris. This is the same kind of perfume the Queen of France wear. That's what he told me. I don't know if it's true or not. I smelled it. It smelled good to me. Here…smell it see if you like it. I was gonna give it to Dolly. But I didn't like her too much.

BERNIECE. *(takes the bottle)* It smells nice.

LYMON. I was gonna give it to Dolly if she had went to the picture with me. Go on, you take it.

BERNIECE. I can't take it. Here…go on, you keep it. You'll find somebody to give it to.

LYMON. I wanna give it to you. Make you smell nice. *(takes the bottle and puts perfume behind* **BERNIECE**'s *ear)* They tell me you supposed to put it right here behind your ear. Say if you put it there you smell nice all day. *(***BERNIECE** *stiffens at his touch. He bends down to smell her.)* There…you smell real good now. *(kisses her neck)* You smell real good for Lymon.

> *(He kisses her again.* **BERNIECE** *returns the kiss, then breaks the embrace and crosses to the stairs. She turns and they look silently at each other.* **LYMON** *hands her the bottle of perfume.* **BERNIECE** *exits up the stairs.* **LYMON** *picks up his suit coat*

*and strokes it lovingly with the full knowledge that
it is indeed a magic suit. The lights go down on
the scene.)*

Scene Four

(It is late the next morning The lights come up on the parlor. **LYMON** *is asleep on the couch.* **BOY WILLIE** *enters through the front door.)*

BOY WILLIE. Hey, Lymon! Lymon, come on, get up.

LYMON. Leave me alone.

BOY WILLIE. Come on, get up, nigger! Wake up, Lymon.

LYMON. What you want?

BOY WILLIE. Come on, let's go. I done called the man about the piano.

LYMON. What piano?

BOY WILLIE. *(dumps* **LYMON** *on the floor)* Come on, get up!

LYMON. Why you leave, I looked around and you was gone.

BOY WILLIE. I come back here with Grace, then I went looking for you. I figured you'd be with Dolly.

LYMON. She just want to drink and spend up your money. I come on back here looking for you to see if you wanted to go to the picture show.

BOY WILLIE. I been up at Grace's house. Some nigger named Leroy come by but I had a chair up against the door. He got mad when he couldn't get in. He went off somewhere and I got out of there before he could come back. Berniece got mad when we came here.

LYMON. She say you was knocking over the lamp busting up the place.

BOY WILLIE. That was Grace doing all that.

LYMON. Wining Boy seen Sutter's ghost last night.

BOY WILLIE. Wining Boy's liable to see anything. I'm surprised he found the right house. Come on, I done called the man about the piano.

LYMON. What he say?

BOY WILLIE. He say to bring it on out. I told him I was calling for my sister, Miss Berniece Charles. I told him some man wanted to buy it for eleven hundred dollars and asked him if he would go any better. He said yeah, he would give me eleven hundred and fifty dollars for it if it was the same piano. I described it to him again and he told me to bring it out.

LYMON. Why didn't you tell him to come and pick it up?

BOY WILLIE. I didn't want to have no problem with Berniece. This way we just take it on out there and it be out the way. He want to charge twenty-five dollars to pick it up.

LYMON. You should have told him the man was gonna give you twelve hundred for it.

BOY WILLIE. I figure I was taking a chance with that eleven hundred. If I had told him twelve hundred he might have run off. Now I wish I had told him twelve-fifty. It's hard to figure out white folks sometimes.

LYMON. You might have been able to tell him anything. White folks got a lot of money.

BOY WILLIE. Come on, let's get it loaded before Berniece come back. Get that end over there. All you got to do is pick it up on that side. Don't worry about this side. You wanna stretch you back for a minute?

LYMON. I'm ready.

BOY WILLIE. Get a real good grip on it now.

(The sound of Sutter's ghost is heard. They do not hear it.)

LYMON. I got this end. You get that end.

BOY WILLIE. Wait till I say ready now. All right. You got it good? You got a grip on it?

LYMON. Yeah, I got it. You lift up on that end.

BOY WILLIE. Ready? Lift!

(The piano will not budge.)

LYMON. Man, this piano is heavy! It's gonna take more than me and you to move this piano.

BOY WILLIE. We can do it. Come on – we did it before.

LYMON. Nigger – you crazy! That piano weighs five hundred pounds!

BOY WILLIE. I got three hundred pounds of it! I know you can carry two hundred pounds! You be lifting them cotton sacks! Come on lift this piano!

(They try to move the piano again without success.)

LYMON. It's stuck. Something holding it.

BOY WILLIE. How the piano gonna be stuck? We just moved it. Slide you end out.

LYMON. Naw – we gonna need two or three more people. How this big old piano get in the house?

BOY WILLIE. I don't know how it got in the house. I know how it's going out though! You get on this end. I'll carry three hundred and fifty pounds of it. All you got to do is slide your end out. Ready?

(They switch sides and try again without success. DOAKER enters from his room as they try to push and shove it.)

LYMON. Hey Doaker...how this piano get in the house?

DOAKER. Boy Willie, what you doing?

BOY WILLIE. I'm carrying this piano out the house. What it look like I'm doing? Come on, Lymon, let's try again.

DOAKER. Go on let the piano sit there till Berniece come home.

BOY WILLIE. You ain't got nothing to do with this, Doaker. This my business.

DOAKER. This is my house, nigger! I ain't gonna let you or nobody else carry nothing out of it. You ain't gonna carry nothing out of here without my permission!

BOY WILLIE. This is my piano. I don't need your permission to carry my belongings out of your house. This is mine. This ain't got nothing to do with you.

DOAKER. I say leave it over there till Berniece come home. She got part of it too. Leave it set there till you see what she say.

BOY WILLIE. I don't care what Berniece say. Come on, Lymon. I got this side.

DOAKER. Go on and cut it half in two if you want to. Just leave Berniece's half sitting over there. I can't tell you what to do with your piano. But I can't let you take her half out of here.

BOY WILLIE. Go on, Doaker. You ain't got nothing to do with this. I don't want you starting nothing now. Just go on and leave me alone. Come on, Lymon. I got this end.

(DOAKER *goes into his room.* BOY WILLIE *and* LYMON *prepare to move the piano.*)

LYMON. How we gonna get it in the truck?

BOY WILLIE. Don't worry about how we gonna get it on the truck. You got to get it out the house first.

LYMON. It's gonna take more than me and you to move this piano.

BOY WILLIE. Just lift up on that end, nigger!

(DOAKER *comes to the doorway of his room and stands.*)

DOAKER. (*quietly, with authority*) Leave that piano set over there till Berniece come back. I don't care what you do with it then. But you gonna leave it sit over there right now.

BOY WILLIE. All right...I'm gonna tell you this, Doaker. I'm going out of here...I'm gonna get me some rope...find me a plank and some wheels...and I'm coming back. Then I'm gonna carry that piano out of here...sell it and give Berniece half the money. See...now that's what I'm gonna do. And you...or nobody else is gonna stop me. Come on, Lymon...let's go get some rope and stuff. I'll be back, Doaker.

(BOY WILLIE *and* LYMON *exit. The lights go down on the scene.*)

Scene Five

*(The lights come up. **BOY WILLIE** sits on the couch, screwing casters on a wooden plank. **MARETHA** is sitting on the piano stool. **DOAKER** sits at the table playing solitaire.)*

BOY WILLIE. *(to **MARETHA**)* Then after that them white folks down around there started falling down their wells. You ever seen a well? A well got a wall around it. It's hard to fall down a well. You got to be leaning way over. Couldn't nobody figure out too much what was making these fellows fall down their well...so everybody says the Ghosts of the Yellow Dog must have pushed them. That's what everybody called them four men what got burned up in the boxcar.

MARETHA. Why they call them that?

BOY WILLIE. 'Cause the Yazoo Delta railroad got yellow boxcars. Sometime the way the whistle blow sound like an old dog howling so the people call it the Yellow Dog.

MARETHA. Anybody ever see the Ghosts?

BOY WILLIE. I told you they like the wind. Can you see the wind?

MARETHA. No.

BOY WILLIE. They like the wind you can't see them. But sometimes you be in trouble they might be around to help you. They say if you go where the Southern cross the Yellow Dog...you go to where them two railroads cross each other...and call out their names...they say they talk back to you. I don't know, I ain't never done that. But Uncle Wining Boy he say he been down there and talked to them. You have to ask him about that part.

*(**BERNIECE** enters through the front door.)*

BERNIECE. Maretha, you go on and get ready for me to do your hair.

*(**MARETHA** crosses to the steps.)*

Boy Willie, I done told you to leave my house. *(to* **MARETHA***)* Go on, Maretha.

*(***MARETHA*** is hesitant about going up the stairs.)*

BOY WILLIE. Don't be scared. Here, I'll go up there with you. If we see Sutter's ghost I'll put a whupping on him. Come on, Uncle Boy Willie going with you.

*(***BOY WILLIE*** and **MARETHA*** exit up the stairs.)*

BERNIECE. Doaker – what is going on here?

DOAKER. I come home and him and Lymon was moving the piano. I told them to leave it over there till you got home. He went out and got that board and them wheels. He say he gonna take that piano out of here and ain't nobody gonna stop him.

BERNIECE. I ain't playing with Boy Willie. I got Crawley's gun upstairs. He don't know but I'm through with it. Where Lymon go?

DOAKER. Boy Willie sent him for some rope just before you come in.

BERNIECE. I ain't studying Boy Willie or Lymon – or the rope. Boy Willie ain't taking that piano out this house. That's all there is to it.

*(***BOY WILLIE*** and **MARETHA*** enter on the stairs. **MARETHA*** carries a hot comb and a can of hair grease. **BOY WILLIE*** comes down and continues to screw the wheels on the board.)*

MARETHA. Mama, all the hair grease is gone. There ain't but this little bit left.

BERNIECE. *(gives her a dollar)* Here…run across the street and get another can. You come straight back, too. Don't you be playing around out there. And watch the cars. Be careful when you cross the street.

*(***MARETHA*** exits out the front door.)*

Boy Willie, I done told you to leave my house.

BOY WILLIE. I ain't in you house. I'm in Doaker's house. If he ask me to leave then I'll go on and leave. But consider me done left your part.

BERNIECE. Doaker, tell him to leave. Tell him to go on.

DOAKER. Boy Willie ain't done nothing for me to put him out of the house. I told you if you can't get along just go on and don't have nothing to do with each other.

BOY WILLIE. I ain't thinking about Berniece. *(gets up and draws a line across the floor with his foot)* There! Now I'm out of your part of the house. Consider me done left your part. Soon as Lymon come back with that rope, I'm gonna take that piano out of here and sell it.

BERNIECE. You ain't gonna touch that piano.

BOY WILLIE. Carry it out of here just as big and bold. Do like my daddy would have done come time to get Sutter's land.

BERNIECE. I got something to make you leave it over there.

BOY WILLIE. It's got to come better than this thirty-two-twenty.

DOAKER. Why don't you stop all that! Boy Willie, go on and leave her alone. You know how Berniece get. Why you wanna sit there and pick with her?

BOY WILLIE. I ain't picking with her. I told her the truth. She the one talking about what she got. I just told her what she better have.

BERNIECE. That's all right, Doaker. Leave him alone.

BOY WILLIE. She trying to scare me. Hell, I ain't scared of dying. I look around and see people dying every day. You got to die to make room for somebody else. I had a dog that died. Wasn't nothing but a puppy. I picked it up and put it in a bag and carried it up there to Reverend C. L. Thompson's church. I carried it up there and prayed and asked Jesus to make it live like he did the man in the Bible. I prayed real hard. Knelt down and everything. Say ask in Jesus' name. Well, I must have called Jesus' name two hundred times. I called his name till my mouth got sore. I got up and looked in the bag and the dog still dead. It ain't moved a muscle! I say, "Well, ain't nothing precious." And then I went out and killed me a cat. That's when I discovered the power of death. See, a nigger that ain't afraid to die is the worse kind of nigger for the white man. He can't hold that power over you. That's what I learned when I killed that cat. I got the power of death too. I can command him. I can call him up. The white man don't like to see that. He don't like for you to stand up and look him square in the eye and say, "I got it too." Then he got to deal with you square up.

BERNIECE. That's why I don't talk to him, Doaker. You try and talk to him and that's the only kind of stuff that comes out his mouth.

DOAKER. You say Avery went home to get his Bible?

BOY WILLIE. What Avery gonna do? Avery can't do nothing with me. I wish Avery would say something to me about this piano.

DOAKER. Berniece ain't said about that. Avery went home to get his Bible. He coming by to bless the house see if he can get rid of Sutter's ghost.

BOY WILLIE. Ain't nothing but a house full of ghosts down there at the church. What Avery look like chasing away somebody's ghost?

(**MARETHA** *enters through the front door.*)

BERNIECE. Light that stove and set that comb over there to get hot. Get something to put around your shoulders.

BOY WILLIE. The Bible say an eye for an eye, a tooth for a tooth, and a life for a life. Tit for tat. But you and Avery don't want to believe that. You gonna pass up that part and pretend it ain't in there. Everything else you gonna agree with. But if you gonna agree with part of it you got to agree with all of it. You can't do nothing halfway. You gonna go at the Bible halfway. You gonna act like that part ain't in there. But you pull out the Bible and open it and see what it say. Ask Avery. He a preacher. He'll tell you it's in there. He the Good Shepherd.

Unless he gonna shepherd you to heaven with half the Bible.

BERNIECE. Maretha, bring me that comb. Make sure it's hot.

(**MARETHA** *brings the comb.* **BERNIECE** *begins to do her hair.*)

BOY WILLIE. I will say this for Avery. He done figured out a path to go through life. I don't agree with it. But he done fixed it so he can go right through it real smooth. Hell, he liable to end up with a million dollars that he done got from selling bread and wine.

MARETHA. OWWWWWW!

BERNIECE. Be still, Maretha. If you was a boy I wouldn't be going through this.

BOY WILLIE. Don't you tell that girl that. Why you wanna tell her that?

BERNIECE. You ain't got nothing to do with this child.

BOY WILLIE. Telling her you wished she was a boy. How's that gonna make her feel?

BERNIECE. Boy Willie, go on and leave me alone.

DOAKER. Why don't you leave her alone? What you got to pick with her for? Why don't you go on out and see what's out there in the streets? Have something to tell the fellows down home.

BOY WILLIE. I'm waiting on Lymon to get back with that truck. Why don't you go on out and see what's out there in the streets? You ain't got to work tomorrow. Talking about me...why don't you go out there? It's Friday night.

DOAKER. I got to stay around here and keep you all from killing one another.

BOY WILLIE. You ain't got to worry about me. I'm gonna be here just as long as it takes Lymon to get back here with that truck. You ought to be talking to Berniece. Sitting up there telling Maretha she wished she was a boy. What kind of thing is that to tell a child? If you want to tell her something tell her about that piano.

You ain't even told her about that piano. Like that's something to be ashamed of. Like she supposed to go off and hide somewhere about that piano. You ought to mark down on the calendar the day that Papa Boy Charles brought that piano into the house. You ought to mark that day down and draw a circle around it… and every year when it come up throw a party. Have a celebration. If you did that she wouldn't have no problem in life. She could walk around here with her head held high. I'm talking about a big party!

Invite everybody! Mark that day down with a special meaning. That way she know where she at in the world. You got her going out here thinking she wrong in the world. Like there ain't no part of it belong to her.

BERNIECE. Let me take care of my child. When you get one of your own then you can teach it what you want to teach it.

(**DOAKER** *exits into his room.*)

BOY WILLIE. What I want to bring a child into this world for? Why I wanna bring somebody else into all this for? I'll tell you this…If I was Rockefeller I'd have forty or fifty. I'd make one every day. 'Cause they gonna start out in life with all the advantages. I ain't got no advantages to offer nobody. Many is the time I looked at my daddy and seen him staring off at his hands. I got a little older I know what he was thinking. He sitting there saying, "I got these big old hands but what I'm gonna do with them? Best I can do is make a fifty-acre crop for Mr. Stovall. Got these big old hands capable of doing anything. I can take and build something with these hands. But where's the tools? All I got is these hands. Unless I go out here and kill me somebody and take what they got…it's a long row to hoe for me to get something of my own. So what I'm gonna do with these big old hands? What would you do?"

See now…if he had his own land he wouldn't have felt that way. If he had something under his feet that belonged to him he could stand up taller. That's what I'm talking about. Hell, the land is there for everybody. All you got to do is figure out how to get you a piece. Ain't no mystery to life. You just got to go out and meet it square on. If you got a piece of land you'll find everything else fall right into place. You can stand right up next to the white man and talk about the price of cotton…the weather, and anything else you want to talk about. If you teach that girl that she living at the bottom of life, she's gonna grow up and hate you.

BERNIECE. I'm gonna teach her the truth. That's just where she living. Only she ain't got to stay there. *(to* MARETHA*)* Turn you head over to the other side.

BOY WILLIE. This might be your bottom but it ain't mine. I'm living at the top of life. I ain't gonna just take my life and throw it away at the bottom. I'm in the world like everybody else. The way I see it everybody else got to come up a little taste to be where I am.

BERNIECE. You right at the bottom with the rest of us.

BOY WILLIE. I'll tell you this…and ain't a living soul can put a comeback on it. If you believe that's where you at then you gonna act that way. If you act that way then that's where you gonna be. It's as simple as that. Ain't no mystery to life. I don't know how you come to believe that stuff. Crawley didn't think like that. He wasn't living at the bottom of life. Papa Boy Charles and Mama Ola wasn't living at the bottom of life. You ain't never heard them say nothing like that. They would have taken a strap to you if they heard you say something like that.

(DOAKER *enters from his room.*)

Hey, Doaker…Berniece say the colored folks is living at the bottom of life. I tried to tell her if she think that… that's where she gonna be. You think you living at the bottom of life? Is that how you see yourself?

DOAKER. I'm just living the best way I know how. I ain't thinking about no top or no bottom.

BOY WILLIE. That's what I tried to tell Berniece. I don't know where she got that from. That sound like something Avery would say. Avery think 'cause the white man give him a turkey for Thanksgiving that makes him better than everybody else. That's gonna raise him out of the bottom of life. I don't need nobody to give me a turkey. I can get my own turkey. All you have to do is get out my way. I'll get me two or three turkeys.

BERNIECE. You can't even get a chicken let alone two or three turkeys. Talking about get out your way. Ain't nobody in your way. *(to* **MARETHA***)* Straighten your head, Maretha! Don't be bending down like that. Hold your head up! *(to* **BOY WILLIE***)* All you got going for you is talk. You whole life that's all you ever had going for you.

BOY WILLIE. See now...I'll tell you something about me. I done strung along and strung along. Going this way and that. Whatever way would lead me to a moment of peace. That's all I want. To be as easy with everything. But I wasn't born to that. I was born to a time of fire. The world ain't wanted no part of me. I could see that since I was about seven. The world say it's better off without me. See, Berniece accept that. She trying to come up to where she can prove something to the world. Hell, the world a better place 'cause of me. I don't see it like Berniece. I got a heart that beats here and it beats just as loud as the next fellow's. Don't care if he black or white. Sometime it beats louder. When it beats louder, then everybody can hear it. Some people get scared of that. Like Berniece. Some people get scared to hear a nigger's heart beating. They think you ought to lay low with that heart. Make it beat quiet and go along with everything the way it is. But my mama ain't birthed me for nothing. So what I got to do? I got to mark my passing on the road. Just like you write on a tree, "Boy Willie was here."

That's all I'm trying to do with that piano. Trying to put my mark on the road. Like my daddy done. My heart say for me to sell that piano and get me some land so I can make a life for myself to live in my own way. Other than that I ain't thinking about nothing Berniece got to say.

> *(There is a knock at the door.* **BOY WILLIE** *crosses to the door and yanks it open thinking it is* **LYMON**. **AVERY** *enters. He carries a Bible.)*

Where you been, nigger? Aw...I thought you was Lymon. Hey, Berniece, look who's here.

BERNIECE. Come on in, Avery. Don't you pay Boy Willie no mind.

BOY WILLIE. Hey...Hey Avery...tell me this...can you get to heaven with half the Bible?

BERNIECE. Boy Willie...I done told you to leave me alone.

BOY WILLIE. I just ask the man a question. He can answer. He don't need you to speak for him. Avery...if you only believe on half the Bible and don't want to accept the other half...you think God let you in heaven? Or do you got to have the whole Bible? Tell Berniece...if you only believe in part of it...when you see God he gonna ask you why you ain't believed in the other part...then he gonna send you straight to hell.

AVERY. You got to be born again. Jesus say "Unless a man be born again he cannot come unto the Father and who so ever heareth my words and believeth them not shall be cast into a fiery pit."

BOY WILLIE. That's what I was trying to tell Berniece. You got to believe in it all. You can't go at nothing halfway. She think she going to heaven with half the Bible. *(to* **BERNIECE***)* You hear that...Jesus say you got to believe in it all.

BERNIECE. You keep messing with me.

BOY WILLIE. I ain't thinking about you.

DOAKER. Come on in, Avery, and have a seat. Don't pay neither one of them no mind. They been arguing all day.

BERNIECE. Come on in, Avery.

AVERY. How's everybody in here?

BERNIECE. *(to* MARETHA*)* Here, set this comb back over there on that stove. *(to* AVERY*)* Don't pay Boy Willie no mind. He been around here bothering me since I come home from work.

BOY WILLIE. Boy Willie ain't bothering you. Boy Willie ain't bothering nobody. I'm just waiting on Lymon to get back. I ain't thinking about you. You heard the man say I was right and you still don't want to believe it. You just wanna go and make up anythin'. Well there's Avery... there's the preacher...go on and ask him.

AVERY. Berniece believe in the Bible. She been baptized.

BOY WILLIE. What about that part that say an eye for an eye a tooth for a tooth and a life for a life? Ain't that in there?

DOAKER. What they say down there at the bank, Avery?

AVERY. Oh, they talked to me real nice. I told Berniece... they say maybe they let me borrow the money. They done talked to my boss down at work and everything.

DOAKER. That's what I told Berniece. You working every day you ought to be able to borrow some money.

AVERY. I'm getting more people in my congregation every day. Berniece says she gonna be the Deaconess. I get me my church I can get married and settled down. That's what I told Berniece.

DOAKER. That be nice. You all ought to go ahead and get married. Berniece don't need to be by herself. I tell her that all the time.

BERNIECE. I ain't said nothing about getting married. I said I was thinking about it.

DOAKER. Avery get him his church you all can make it nice. *(to* AVERY*)* Berniece said you was coming by to bless the house.

AVERY. Yeah, I done read up on my Bible. She asked me to come by and see if I can get rid of Sutter's ghost.

BOY WILLIE. Ain't no ghost in this house. That's all in Berniece's head. Go on up there and see if you see him.

I'll give you a hundred dollars if you see him. That's all in her imagination.

DOAKER. Well, let her find that out then. If Avery blessing the house is gonna make her feel better...what you got to do with it?

AVERY. Berniece say Maretha seen him too. I don't know, but I found a part in the Bible to bless the house. If he is here then that ought to make him go.

BOY WILLIE. You worse than Berniece believing all that stuff. Talking about...if he here. Go on up there and find out. I been up there I ain't seen him. If you reading from that Bible gonna make him leave out of Berniece imagination, well, you might be right. But if you talking about –

DOAKER. Boy Willie, why don't you just be quiet? Getting all up in the man's business. This ain't got nothing to do with you. Let him go ahead and do what he gonna do.

BOY WILLIE. I ain't stopping him. Avery ain't got no power to do nothing.

AVERY. Oh, I ain't got no power. God got the power! God got power over everything in his creation. God can do anything. God say, "As I commandeth so it shall be." God said, "Let there be light," and there was light. He made the world in six days and rested on the seventh. God's got a wonderful power. He got power over life and death. Jesus raised Lazarus from the dead. They was getting ready to bury him and Jesus told him say, "Rise up and walk." He got up and walked and the people made great rejoicing at the power of God. I ain't worried about him chasing away a little old ghost!

(*There is a knock at the door.* **BOY WILLIE** *goes to answer it.* **LYMON** *enters carrying a coil of rope.*)

BOY WILLIE. Where you been? I been waiting on you and you run off somewhere.

LYMON. I ran into Grace. I stopped and bought her drink. She say she gonna go to the picture show with me.

BOY WILLIE. I ain't thinking about no Grace nothing.

LYMON. Hi, Berniece.

BOY WILLIE. Give me that rope and get up on this side of the piano.

DOAKER. Boy Willie, don't start nothing now. Leave the piano alone.

BOY WILLIE. Get that board there, Lymon. Stay out of this, Doaker.

(BERNIECE *exits up the stairs.*)

DOAKER. You just can't take the piano. How you gonna take the piano? Berniece ain't said nothing about selling that piano.

BOY WILLIE. She ain't got to say nothing. Come on, Lymon. We got to lift one end at a time up on the board. You got to watch so that the board don't slide up under there.

LYMON. What we gonna do with the rope?

BOY WILLIE. Let me worry about the rope. You just get up on this side over here with me.

(BERNIECE *enters from the stairs. She has her hand in her pocket where she has Crawley's gun.*)

AVERY. Boy Willie…Berniece…why don't you all sit down and talk this out now?

BERNIECE. Ain't nothing to talk out.

BOY WILLIE. I'm through talking to Berniece. You can talk to Berniece till you get blue in the face, and it don't make no difference. Get up on that side, Lymon. Throw that rope around there and tie it to the leg.

LYMON. Wait a minute…wait a minute, Boy Willie. Berniece got to say. Hey, Berniece…did you tell Boy Willie he could take this piano?

BERNIECE. Boy Willie ain't taking nothing out of my house but himself. Now you let him go ahead and try.

BOY WILLIE. Come on, Lymon, get up on this side with me.

(**LYMON** *stands undecided.*)

Come on, nigger! What you standing there for?

LYMON. Maybe Berniece is right, Boy Willie. Maybe you shouldn't sell it.

AVERY. You all ought to sit down and talk it out. See if you can come to an agreement.

DOAKER. That's what I been trying to tell them. Seem like one of them ought to respect the other one's wishes.

BERNIECE. I wish Boy Willie would go on and leave my house. That's what I wish. Now, he can respect that. 'Cause he's leaving here one way or another.

BOY WILLIE. What you mean one way or another? What's that supposed to mean? I ain't scared of no gun.

DOAKER. Come on, Berniece, leave him alone with that.

BOY WILLIE. I don't care what Berniece say. I'm selling my half. I can't help it if her half got to go along with it. It ain't like I'm trying to cheat her out of her half. Come on, Lymon.

LYMON. Berniece...I got to do this...Boy Willie say he gonna give you half of the money...say he want to get Sutter's land.

BERNIECE. Go on, Lymon. Just go on...I done told Boy Willie what to do.

BOY WILLIE. Here, Lymon...put that rope up over there.

LYMON. Boy Willie, you sure you want to do this? The way I figure it...I might be wrong...but I figure she gonna shoot you first.

BOY WILLIE. She just gonna have to shoot me.

BERNIECE. Maretha, get on out the way. Get her out the way, Doaker.

DOAKER. Go on, do what your mama told you.

BERNIECE. Put her in your room.

(**MARETHA** *exits to* **DOAKER**'s *room.* **BOY WILLIE** *and* **LYMON** *try to lift the piano. The door opens and* **WINING BOY** *enters. He has been drinking.*)

WINING BOY. Man, these niggers around here! I stopped down there at Seefus…These folks standing around talking about Patchneck Red's coming. They jumping back and getting off the sidewalk talking about Patchneck Red this and Patchneck Red that. Come to find out…you know who they was talking about? Old John D. from up around Tyler! Used to run around with Otis Smith. He got everybody scared of him. Calling him Patchneck Red. They don't know I whupped the nigger's head in one time.

BOY WILLIE. Just make sure that board don't slide, Lymon.

LYMON. I got this side. You watch that side.

WINING BOY. Hey, Boy Willie, what you got? I know you got a pint stuck up in your coat.

BOY WILLIE. Wining Boy, get out the way!

WINING BOY. Hey, Doaker. What you got? Gimme a drink. I want a drink.

DOAKER. It look like you had enough of whatever it was. Come talking about, "What you got?" You ought to be trying to find somewhere to lay down.

WINING BOY. I ain't worried about no place to lay down. I can always find me a place to lay down in Berniece's house. Ain't that right, Berniece?

BERNIECE. Wining Boy, sit down somewhere. You been out there drinking all day. Come in here smelling like an old polecat. Sit on down there, you don't need nothing to drink.

DOAKER. You know Berniece don't like all that drinking.

WINING BOY. I ain't disrespecting Berniece. Berniece, am I disrespecting you? I'm just trying to be nice. I been with strangers all day and they treated me like family. I come in here to family and you treat me like a stranger. I don't need your whiskey. I can buy my own. I wanted your company, not your whiskey.

DOAKER. Nigger, why don't you go upstairs and lay down? You don't need nothing to drink.

WINING BOY. I ain't thinking about no laying down. Me and Boy Willie fixing to party. Ain't that right, Boy Willie? Tell him. I'm fixing to play me some piano. Watch this.

(**WINING BOY** *sits down at the piano.*)

BOY WILLIE. Come on, Wining Boy! Me and Lymon fixing to move the piano.

WINING BOY. Wait a minute…wait a minute. This a song I wrote for Cleotha. I wrote this song in memory of Cleotha.

(*begins to play and sing:*)

HEY LITTLE WOMAN WHAT'S THE MATTER WITH YOU NOW
HAD A STORM LAST NIGHT AND BLOWED THE LINE ALL DOWN

TELL ME HOW LONG
IS I GOT TO WAIT
CAN I GET IT NOW
OR MUST I HESITATE

IT TAKES A HESITATING STOCKING IN HER HESITATING SHOE
IT TAKES A HESITATING WOMAN WANNA SING THE BLUES

TELL ME HOW LONG
IS I GOT TO WAIT
CAN I KISS YOU NOW
OR MUST I HESITATE.

BOY WILLIE. Come on, Wining Boy, get up! Get up, Wining Boy! Me and Lymon's fixing to move the piano.

WINING BOY. Naw…Naw…you ain't gonna move this piano!

BOY WILLIE. Get out the way, Wining Boy.

(**WINING BOY**, *his back to the piano, spreads his arms out over the piano.*)

WINING BOY. You ain't taking this piano out the house. You got to take me with it!

BOY WILLIE. Get on out the way, Wining Boy! Doaker, get him!

(There is a knock on the door.)

BERNIECE. I got him, Doaker. Come on, Wining Boy. I done told Boy Willie he ain't taking the piano.

> **(BERNIECE** *tries to take* **WINING BOY** *away from the piano.)*

WINING BOY. He got to take me with it!

> **(DOAKER** *goes to answer the door.* **GRACE** *enters.)*

GRACE. Is Lymon here?

DOAKER. Lymon.

WINING BOY. He ain't taking that piano.

BERNIECE. I ain't gonna let him take it.

GRACE. I thought you was coming back. I ain't gonna sit in that truck all day.

LYMON. I told you I was coming back.

GRACE. *(sees* BOY WILLIE*)* Oh, hi, Boy Willie. Lymon told me you was gone back down South.

LYMON. I said he was going back. I didn't say he had left already.

GRACE. That's what you told me.

BERNIECE. Lymon, you got to take your company someplace else.

LYMON. Berniece, this is Grace. That there is Berniece. That's Boy Willie's sister.

GRACE. Nice to meet you. *(to* **LYMON***)* I ain't gonna sit out in that truck all day. You told me you was gonna take me to the movie.

LYMON. I told you I had something to do first. You supposed to wait on me.

BERNIECE. Lymon, just go on and leave. Take Grace or whoever with you. Just go on get out my house.

BOY WILLIE. You gonna help me move this piano first, nigger!

LYMON. *(to* GRACE*)* I got to help Boy Willie move the piano first.

(Everybody but **GRACE** *suddenly senses Sutter's presence.)*

GRACE. I ain't waiting on you. Told me you was coming right back. Now you got to move a piano. You just like all the other men.

*(***GRACE*** now senses something.)*

Something ain't right here. I knew I shouldn't have come back up in this house.

*(***GRACE*** exits.)*

LYMON. Hey Grace! I'll be right back, Boy Willie.

BOY WILLIE. Where you going, nigger?

LYMON. I'll be back. I got to take Grace home.

BOY WILLIE. Come on, let's move the piano first!

LYMON. I got to take Grace home. I told you I'll be back.

*(***LYMON*** exits. ***BOY WILLIE*** exits and calls after him.)*

BOY WILLIE. Come on, Lymon! Hey...Lymon! Lymon... come on!

(Again, the presence of Sutter is felt.)

WINING BOY. Hey, Doaker, did you feel that? Hey, Berniece...did you get cold? Hey, Doaker...

DOAKER. What you calling me for?

WINING BOY. I believe that's Sutter.

DOAKER. Well, let him stay up there. As long as he don't mess with me.

BERNIECE. Avery, go on and bless the house.

DOAKER. You need to bless that piano. That's what you need to bless. It ain't done nothing but cause trouble. If you gonna bless anything go on and bless that.

WINING BOY. Hey Doaker, if he gonna bless something let him bless everything. The kitchen...the upstairs. Go on and bless it all.

BOY WILLIE. Ain't no ghost in this house. He need to bless Berniece's head. That's what he need to bless.

AVERY. Seem like that piano's causing all the trouble. I can bless that. Berniece, put me some water in that bottle.

> (**AVERY** *takes a small bottle from his pocket and hands it to* **BERNIECE**, *who goes into the kitchen to get water.* **AVERY** *takes a candle from his pocket and lights it. He gives it to* **BERNIECE** *as she gives him the water.*)

Hold this candle. Whatever you do make sure it don't go out.

O Holy Father we gather here this evening in the Holy Name to cast out the spirit of one James Sutter. May this vial of water be empowered with thy spirit. May each drop of it be a weapon and a shield against the presence of all evil and may it be a cleansing and blessing of this humble abode.

Just as Our Father taught us how to pray so He say, "I will prepare a table for you in the midst of mine enemies," and in His hands we place ourselves to come unto his presence. Where there is Good so shall it cause Evil to scatter to the Four Winds.

> (*He throws water at the piano at each commandment.*)

Get thee behind me, Satan! Get thee behind the face of Righteousness as we Glorify His Holy Name! Get thee behind the Hammer of Truth that breaketh down the Wall of Falsehood! Father. Father. Praise. Praise. We ask in Jesus' name and call forth the power of the Holy Spirit as it is written…(*opens the Bible and reads from it*) "I will sprinkle clean water upon thee and ye shall be clean."

BOY WILLIE. All this old preaching stuff. Hell, just tell him to leave.

> (**AVERY** *continues reading throughout* **BOY WILLIE***'s outburst.*)

AVERY. "I will sprinkle clean water upon you and you shall be clean: from all your uncleanliness, and from all your idols, will I cleanse you. A new heart also will I give you, and a new spirit will I put within you: and I will take out of your flesh the heart of stone, and I will give you a heart of flesh. And I will put my spirit within you, and cause you to walk in my statutes, and ye shall keep my judgments, and do them."

(BOY WILLIE grabs a pot of water from the stove and begins to fling it around the room.)

BOY WILLIE. Hey Sutter! Sutter! Get your ass out this house! Sutter! Come on and get some of this water! You done drowned in the well, come on and get some more of this water!

(BOY WILLIE is working himself into a frenzy as he runs around the room throwing water and calling Sutter's name. AVERY continues reading.)

Come on, Sutter! *(starts up the stairs)* Come on, get some water! Come on, Sutter!

(The sound of Sutter's Ghost is heard. As BOY WILLIE moves up the stairs he is suddenly thrown back by the unseen force, which is choking him. As he struggles, he frees himself, then dashes up the stairs.)

Come on, Sutter!

AVERY. *(continuing)* "A new heart also will I give you and a new spirit will I put within you: and I will take out of your flesh the heart of stone, and I will give you a heart of flesh. And I will put my spirit within you, and cause you to walk in my statutes, and ye shall keep my judgments, and do them."

(There are loud sounds heard from upstairs as BOY WILLIE begins to wrestle with Sutter's ghost. It is a life-and-death struggle fraught with perils and faultless terror. BOY WILLIE is thrown down the stairs. AVERY is stunned into silence. BOY WILLIE picks himself up and dashes back upstairs.)

Berniece, I can't do it.

(There are more sounds heard from upstairs. **DOAKER** *and* **WINING BOY** *stare at one another in stunned disbelief. It is in this moment, from somewhere old, that* **BERNIECE** *realizes what she must do. She crosses to the piano. She begins to play. The song is found piece by piece. It is an old urge to song that is both a commandment and a plea. With each repetition it gains in strength. It is intended as an exorcism and a dressing for battle. A rustle of wind blowing across two continents.)*

BERNIECE. *(singing)*
    I WANT YOU TO HELP ME
    I WANT YOU TO HELP ME
    I WANT YOU TO HELP ME
    I WANT YOU TO HELP ME
    I WANT YOU TO HELP ME
    I WANT YOU TO HELP ME
    MAMA BERNIECE

    I WANT YOU TO HELP ME
    MAMA ESTHER
    I WANT YOU TO HELP ME
    PAPA BOY CHARLES
    I WANT YOU TO HELP ME
    MAMA OLA
    I WANT YOU TO HELP ME

    I WANT YOU TO HELP ME
    I WANT YOU TO HELP ME
    I WANT YOU TO HELP ME
    I WANT YOU TO HELP ME
    I WANT YOU TO HELP ME
    I WANT YOU TO HELP ME
    I WANT YOU TO HELP ME
    I WANT YOU TO HELP ME.

    (The sound of a train approaching is heard. The noise upstairs subsides.)

BOY WILLIE. Come on, Sutter! Come back, Sutter!

    *(***BERNIECE*** begins to chant.)*

BERNIECE. Thank you.

Thank you.

Thank you.

> *(A calm comes over the house.* **MARETHA** *enters from* **DOAKER**'s *room.* **BOY WILLIE** *enters on the stairs. He pauses a moment to watch* **BERNIECE** *at the piano.)*

Thank you.

Thank you.

BOY WILLIE. Wining Boy, you ready to go back down home? Hey, Doaker, what time the train leave?

DOAKER. You still got time to make it.

> *(***MARETHA** *crosses and embraces* **BOY WILLIE**.*)*

BOY WILLIE. Hey Berniece…if you and Maretha don't keep playing on that piano…ain't no telling…me and Sutter both liable to be back.

> *(He exits.)*

BERNIECE. Thank you.

> *(The lights fade to black.)*

End of Play

August Wilson

(April 27, 1945 – October 2, 2005)

August Wilson authored *Gem of the Ocean, Joe Turner's Come and Gone, Ma Rainey's Black Bottom, The Piano Lesson, Seven Guitars, Fences, Two Trains Running, Jitney, King Hedley II* and *Radio Golf.* These works explore the heritage and experience of African Americans, decade by decade, over the course of the twentieth century. Mr. Wilson's plays have been produced at regional theaters across the country, on Broadway and throughout the world. In 2003, Mr. Wilson made his professional stage debut in his one-man show *How I Learned What I Learned.*

Mr. Wilson's work garnered many awards, including the Pulitzer Prize for *Fences* (1987) and *The Piano Lesson* (1990); a Tony Award for *Fences*; Great Britain's Olivier Award for *Jitney*; and eight New York Drama Critics Circle awards for *Ma Rainey's Black Bottom, Fences, Joe Turner's Come and Gone, The Piano Lesson, Two Trains Running, Seven Guitars, Jitney* and *Radio Golf.* Additionally, the cast recording of *Ma Rainey's Black Bottom* received a 1985 Grammy Award, and Mr. Wilson received a 1995 Emmy Award nomination for his screenplay adaptation of *The Piano Lesson.* Mr. Wilson's early works include the one-act plays: *The Janitor, Recycle, The Coldest Day of the Year, Malcolm X, The Homecoming* and the musical satire *Black Bart and the Sacred Hills.*

Mr. Wilson received many fellowships and awards, including Rockefeller and Guggenheim fellowships in playwriting, the Whiting Writers Award and the 2003 Heinz Award. He was awarded a 1999 National Humanities Medal by the President of the United States, and received numerous honorary degrees from colleges and universities, as well as the only high school diploma ever issued by the Carnegie Library of Pittsburgh.

He was an alumnus of New Dramatists, a member of the American Academy of Arts and Sciences, a 1995 inductee into the American Academy of Arts and Letters, and on October 16, 2005, Broadway renamed the theater located at 245 West 52nd Street: The August Wilson Theatre. In 2007, he was posthumously inducted into the Theater Hall of Fame.

Mr. Wilson was born and raised in the Hill District of Pittsburgh, and lived in Seattle at the time of his death. He is survived by two daughters, Sakina Ansari and Azula Carmen Wilson, and his wife, costume designer Constanza Romero.